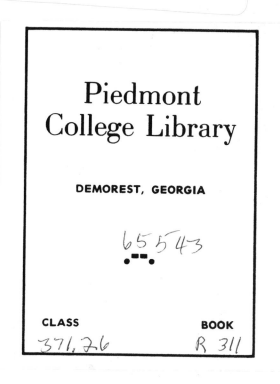

Research Strategies for Evaluating Training

AMERICAN EDUCATIONAL RESEARCH ASSOCIATION
MONOGRAPH SERIES
ON
CURRICULUM EVALUATION

American Educational Research Association
1126 Sixteenth Street, N. W.
Washington, D. C. 20036

Research Strategies
for Evaluating Training

Edited by

Philip H. DuBois
Washington University
St. Louis, Missouri

G. Douglas Mayo
Naval Air Station
Millington, Tennessee

Rand McNally & Company
Chicago

Rand McNally Education Series
B. Othanel Smith, *Advisory Editor*

American Educational Research Association
Monograph Series on Curriculum Evaluation

10/26/71 p.l. 3-50

Contents

LIST OF FIGURES

LIST OF TABLES

Research Strategies for Evaluating Training

INTRODUCTION

The point is often made that in such complex areas as curriculum evaluation there must be sustained effort over a period of years if substantial progress is to be made. With this thought in mind, the Office of Naval Research in 1952 began a contract with Washington University of St. Louis to develop and test research strategies for evaluating training. At the time of the publication of this monograph this contract is still in force. Its first two years were under the direction of Wilse B. Webb, and since then, the principal investigator has been Philip H. DuBois. The underlying thought is that Navy training, and education in general, can profit from a project wherein the principal investigator is given a broad charter to develop research strategy for evaluation, with access to a training situation which is complex in terms of subjects and freedom to manipulate experimental variables. Most of the research under the contract has been accomplished at the Naval Air Technical Training Command headquartered at Millington, Tennessee.

The project provides for one man, usually a graduate student working on a Ph.D. dissertation, to be in residence at the training site. This research psychologist, while working exclusively on contract matters, becomes for practical purposes also a part of the Naval Air Technical Training Command organization for training research. This organization was headed throughout the period in question by G. Douglas Mayo.

Under the direction of the principal investigator, graduate students working at Millington have produced six Ph.D. dissertations, in addition to two masters theses and a number of technical reports. Some of the papers in the present monograph are based upon these theses and dissertations.

From time to time, as it has appeared useful, a conference has been called to integrate accomplishments and to air the views of consultants from other Navy research organizations and from universities. In all, seven of these conferences have been held. Lasting two days, they have normally involved 16 to 20 participants. Programs have consisted of theoretical and research papers stemming from work recently completed by the project, papers on related topics by consultants and Navy training research personnel, consideration of papers by selected discussants, and general discussion. Selections for the present monograph have been made from the papers presented at these conferences. When the comments of a discussant appeared to be of special pertinence, they have been included immediately following the paper.

The primary purpose of the AERA series is to encourage scholarly study of, and to improve technical practice in, the evaluation of education. The first issue of the monograph series, *Perspectives in Curric-*

1

ulum Evaluation, set forth the need for new methodology, with emphasis on task analysis, content validity, diagnostic testing, and mastery testing. The role of judgment and formative and summative evaluation also was delineated. To a degree, the first issue of the monograph series goes beyond a description of the problems involved and points the way to solutions. However, in setting the tone for subsequent issues it was neither feasible nor desirable to give detailed consideration to all of the problem areas that were identified. The present monograph attempts to go into greater detail in one of these areas, that of research strategies and topics closely related to it. An effort has been made to select papers that are pertinent at the present time. The sole purpose of the monograph is to be useful to individuals engaged in education and training, and research in these areas; it is not intended as an historical documentation of the Navy project on research strategies in training.

Since the goals of education and training as stated by different individuals and groups usually involve change, a major part of the project on research strategies for evaluating training, and a substantial proportion of the individual papers in the present monograph, focus on the measurement of change.

The monograph is organized into three main parts, each consisting of four to six papers. Each part is preceded by an introduction by the editors. Part I, "Basic Issues in Training Research," aims at a more encompassing view of research strategy than the other two parts, and thus is similar to the first monograph in the curriculum evaluation series. However, there is little overlap in terms of actual content. Part II, "Measurement of Learning," delineates the central problems with which the monograph is concerned, including a number of problems of long standing, such as the problems of the criterion and of the reliability of measuring instruments. Part III, "Methods and Results," presents much of the constructive work that has been accomplished by the research strategies project. A major portion of this work centers around the adaptation and application of correlational analysis to practical training evaluation problems.

As noted by Stake in the introduction to Monograph #1, curriculum evaluation differs from educational research in its orientation to a specific program rather than to variables common to many programs. But research and evaluation share many methods. The content of the present monograph is drawn from the province of educational research, with the hope and expectation that these strategies will be applicable for the evaluation of a wide spectrum of educational and training programs.

PART I

Basic Issues in Training Research

As noted by Stake (1967) in the first monograph in this series, there is a hierarchy of dependency in educational evaluation. At the functional level, standard operating procedures are needed, but the criteria for adequate procedures require rationales, which ultimately depend upon theories. Thus, the basic issues are theoretical and rational in nature, and normally precede the criterion and procedural aspects of training research.

Even in training in organizations as functionally oriented as the military and industry, a single concept has effected great change in recent years. This concept sprang originally from Skinner's operant behaviorism but evolved within a few years to a functionally autonomous status; now it is only marginally related to any explicit theory of learning. The concept is that of validated instruction. Much has been written that relates to this concept, including a paper by Gagné (1967) in the first monograph of this series. The essential elements of validated instruction are: analysis of the tasks the student is expected to perform following training, statement of the terminal behaviors that jointly make up the tasks, measurement of these terminal behaviors, and revision of the resulting instructional material until performance specifications are met. Thus, instruction is validated in much the same way that tests have been validated for many years.

Why has it taken so long to conceive and apply this simple concept to training? Doubtless, one of the primary reasons is the low reliability of instruction, in the test-retest sense of the term. Relatively recent developments in standardized packaging of instruction in the form of programmed instruction booklets, educational television tapes, computer-assisted instruction programs, and recorded audiovisual presentations have gone a long way toward solving the reliability problem in the preparation of validated instructional material. In addition to advantages these media offer from the standpoint of test-retest reliability, they stabilize instruction during the validation process and freeze it in the revised form after validation has been accomplished. It is true that systematic procedures to guide one through the essential elements of validated instruction leave much to be desired, but few who have attempted seriously to apply the concept of validated instruction have found the associated procedures so inadequate as to warrant dismissing the concept as impractical.

In industrial and military training validated instruction has become a tide that at this time is running strong. It seems clear that it is not a fad, since there is little question that the mark being made by validated instruction is quite indelible.

A second concept that is of major importance to training is not at all new, but, unlike validated instruction, has not yet made a significant impact upon the way in which training is carried out. This is the concept of individualized instruction. The doctrine of individual differences needs no elaboration here. However, with few exceptions the application of measured differences between individuals has been in the form of assignment of the individual to a training group. Only rarely has individualized training been available which permitted finer tuning to individual aptitudes and needs than is possible by assignment to one of several groups. Training becomes much the same for everyone once he is within the group.

Individualized instruction envisions a major change in all of this. It envisions a training system which is not only individually paced throughout, but one in which both the content and level of instructional material are selected in accordance with the most effective means of guiding each individual from his initial position with respect to certain behaviors or capabilities to the desired position.

The desirability of individualized training has been recognized for quite a long while, but with a few exceptions, such as college tutorials, small group instruction in the primary grades, and one-to-one instructor-student ratios in flight training and in apprenticeship training, we have not had a practical means of implementing individualized training. As in the case of validated instruction, relatively new means of packaging instruction for individualized instruction seem to point the way toward achievement of this goal. In large-scale training operations individualized instruction engenders complexities which can hardly be handled except by a computer.

Two leading roles are currently proposed for the computer in individualized training. In time, these roles may well merge into one. The first is tutorial computer-assisted instruction, which simulates a one-to-one instructor-student ratio. Instruction in this mode requires that the student be on-line with the computer at all times, since he is in a constant dialog with the computer. The computer may supplement the tutorial function with such functions as information retrieval, computation, and simulation. The second role proposed for the computer involves the student's being routed through the course by the computer, but receiving most of his instruction off-line by means of units or modules of instruction packaged according to any one of several modes of individual instruction. In this system adaptation may be built into the unit of instruction by such means as branching or remedial loops in programmed instruction, or audiovisual and other materials may be written at several different levels of difficulty or depth to adjust to measured differences among individual students. In this system, which is sometimes referred to as computer-managed instruction, the computer may also be programmed to make optimal use of resources thereby reducing the need for individualized audiovisual devices, other training equipment, and laboratory and shop space.

What is the relationship between these two concepts, validated instruction and individualized instruction? Can one exist without the other? The relationship is one of partial interdependency. Validated instruction certainly can be given in a group situation. Nearly all of it at the present time is given in this situation. It cannot, however, attain its maximum value in a group setting since students who quickly achieve the desired terminal performance must wait for the remainder of the class to catch up. Similarly, individualized instruction does not have to be validated. Instructional material which is intended to be adaptive to a wide range of individual differences in students can be written completely a priori, and with none of the characteristics of validated instruction. But almost without exception, individualized instruction will be more effective if it is also validated instruction.

The four papers which follow in this section view the basic issues in training research from different vantage points, and understandably address themselves to different facets of the problem. The above discussion of two current and prominent concepts in training represents still another facet and is intended to supplement rather than elaborate upon the excellent papers that follow. Preceding each paper, however, there are brief editorial comments.

Strategy of Research on Learning in Educational Settings

James M. Vanderplas

Washington University

[Vanderplas loses no time in identifying the problem that research pertaining to training methods has been neither as extensive nor as productive as one reasonably might expect. He
carefully analyzes the causes and, in part, from these causes de-
rives a strategy that may hold considerable promise for increasing productivity of research in practical educational situations.
Central to this strategy is the development and exploration of
hypotheses concerning the relationship between principles of
learning and principles of education. The difference between
these principles becomes clear when we note that Vanderplas
envisions an intermediate situation, midway between the laboratory and the classroom, in which research in human learning
would be conducted. In this setting intermediate principles would
be developed which would be both consistent with learning
theory and applicable in the educational setting.]

Three pressing and serious problems facing education today are: ris-
ing student enrollments, inadequate classroom space, and the shortage
of qualified teachers. These problems are being met by efforts in three
directions: first of all by crash programs of expansion and more efficient
use of existing classroom facilities, secondly by attracting and training
more teachers, and thirdly by the search for better methods of train-

ing. Research designed to find more effective training methods has only recently received attention and support on a major scale.

This relative neglect of research on training methods has occurred for three reasons: first, the educational community for most of its history has been concerned with organizational, structural, and administrative problems which, by their very nature, preclude systematic research into methods: problems of how best to organize the school for effective management of the student, problems of how to organize the sequence of material to be compatible with natural growth and of managing students' classroom activities for compatibility with the extracurricular social context. Once an organizational framework and a management policy have been rigidly fixed, the necessary flexibility for research on training methods is lost. To the extent that related work on teaching methods is considered, it takes the form of relatively unstructured searches for effective teacher qualities or conduct, described in terms such as enthusiasm, motivation, supportive behavior, knowledge of the pupil, and ability to stimulate. But, while teacher-related qualities are important, just as are managerial characteristics, the preoccupation with searches in these directions has done little to advance training methods as such.

The second reason for the neglect of research on methods relates to the natural reluctance of educators to regard methods variables independently of teacher and pupil variables, and with their tendency to regard the goals of education within a context too broad to encompass the moment-by-moment achievements of the pupil during the daily classroom activities. One finds as educational goals not skills such as arithmetic, spelling, reading and comprehension, speech, and musical skill but high sounding and vague goals such as education of the whole child, education for democracy, civic responsibility, and self-realization. As one prominent educational writer has pointed out, such broadly stated goals usually result in aimless daily activity by the teacher and little specific achievement by the pupil. The good teacher, by these vague criteria, is one who fosters student activity toward vague goals, helps the child to use his natural talents in gaining skills, and motivates him to study. The good teacher might not at all be one who manages *for* the child his daily drill assignments in spelling, with specific reinforcement of desired behavior, guidance of arithmetic skill development, and direction of his moment-by-moment activities in tested ways to bring about his attainment of specific lesson outcomes. By keeping our sights on broad, long-term goals, and by emphasizing the interactive characteristics of teacher-pupil-method variables, we may well overlook and fail to provide the *methods* which might be used on good and poor students alike, by good and not-so-good teachers equally, and by which we satisfy specific, short-term goals important in attaining the broad, long-term ones.

The third reason for neglect of research on methods is easier to describe, and it has to do with a confusion of tools, materials, and media with methods and techniques. This confusion was brought out quite clearly in a recent speech by a vice-president of the Ford Motor Company to the National School Board Association at St. Louis. Among other pronouncements having to do with inefficient use of classroom and laboratory space, student-teacher ratio, and the semester system, he pointed out that live or taped television systems can be used to teach upwards of 150 to 200 students at a time. But few schools, he said, are exploiting this new teaching technique! Now, live or taped TV is admittedly an excellent *medium* for the propagation of information, i.e., an excellent mass communication medium; but to confuse it with a *method* of teaching is to commit a fundamental error of both pedagogy and the psychology of learning. Not only does the teacher lose completely the necessary contact with the student, which in most subjects is required for detailed supervision, but also the teacher and the pupil lose an important part of the interaction necessary for effective management of the student's progress, including reinforcement, scheduling of concepts, participation and recitation, and other factors shown both in laboratory studies and in the classroom to be of crucial importance. At best, the use of such techniques assumes wrongly that no individual differences exist among students, that participation is unnecessary, and that all students profit equally from hearing a taped message without knowing if they have learned from it.

Similar confusion of media, materials, and tools may be seen in typical textbooks on teaching principles. In one, for example, an entire chapter is devoted to the concept of *drill* as a technique of teaching. Now drill, in the common sense use of the term, may vaguely resemble a technique, in that it involves repetitive practice under controlled supervision, but I would suggest that drill as such is a means of organization and not a method of teaching—that is, it is more like group discussion, lecture, participation, or television as a concept, than like distribution of practice, immediate reward, or selection of common elements for transfer, and other detailed procedures which may be manipulated and varied in the process of drill. While our representative text writer correctly distinguishes rote, unenlightened, unreinforced, and boring repetitive responses from skillfully guided behavior during practice with appropriate and immediate reinforcement of correct behavior, his treatment of drill as an overall method or technique serves more, in my opinion, to confuse the issue than to clarify and develop a teaching method.

My major point is that we need to distinguish more sharply between media, tools, and materials on one hand and methods on the other, if research on methods is to be effectively carried out.

In seeking better methods of training, one might turn to the psychology of learning to find, hopefully, fundamental principles of learning which would bear on the problem of training. At least, in the absence of clear and uncontroversial principles, generalizations might be made from laboratory studies of learning to classroom activities of training. However, this does not seem to be easy.

Most educators would not agree that the principles of learning, developed in laboratory settings, are easily translated into principles directly applicable to the tasks of training encountered in the classroom. Many would even deny that such direct translation is possible, now or in the future. Although some psychologists, on the other hand, would stoutly defend the principles in spite of this inability to translate them directly, we cannot overlook the fact that large gaps are numerous. Let me illustrate one or two, taken from a recent paper by Robert Gagné (1962), a psychologist concerned with problems of training. Gagné points out that in many complex tasks the well-known principles of learning, such as repetition, knowledge of results, distribution of practice, similarity, familiarity, and distinctiveness of cues are difficult, if not impossible, to identify and use in a practical way. In learning gunnery, for example, sheer repetitive practice, even with knowledge of results, is not a particularly effective training method. Instruction about the correct sighting picture for ranging seems to be much more effective in bringing about improvement. Similarly, variation in practice and rest periods during learning did not, in one study, bring about corresponding variations in learning of the gunnery task. Similarity relations, cue distinctiveness, and familiarity were also found to be ineffective.

On the basis of these findings, Gagné raises doubts about the usefulness of assumed learning principles and prefers to look to such techniques as task analysis and to principles of component analysis, intra-task transfer, and sequencing of subtasks to find ideas of greater usefulness in design of learning situations. Gagné thus illustrates that learning a complex task such as gunnery, in a complex setting, may require a different level of principle than that required by a simpler task in a simpler setting, such as a laboratory.

More traditionally minded theorists, such as Kenneth Spence, would argue that a science of learning, to be applicable to the problems of training, must build upon the principles worked out in simple settings. As more principles develop and increase in applicability, we should expect to find them more powerful, once they are applied, in explaining how training may be designed.

Others, such as B. F. Skinner, would argue that educators have missed the boat—that they have ignored the exquisite detail into which behaviors must be shaped if they are to be improved—and would emphasize the need for programmed instruction or for the use of teaching machines.

I think both of these approaches are incorrect. Spence would have us wait until the laboratory is developed into a classroom, perhaps much too late; Skinner would have us bring the student from the classroom to the laboratory, or turn the classroom into a mass production, laboratory assembly line.

I believe that the correct answer lies in a strategy between these extremes. I believe that it would be possible to develop intermediate principles which are consistent with learning theory and applicable to the educational setting, and that an effective strategy of research could be formulated which would bring to bear the principles of reinforcement, distribution of practice, distinctiveness, response availability, and so on, upon problems of training. One such intermediate principle, related to reinforcement at the one extreme and to knowledge of results at the other, is the principle of *feedback*. Feedback resembles reinforcement in that it is a process whereby the subject gains information about the correctness of his behavior. It resembles knowledge of results in that it provides him with information about the relation of the behavior to his motives, goals, and progress toward the goals. Feedback differs from reinforcement in that it may be defined as any consequence of behavior. This definition is independent of the behavior and does not depend upon its relation to drive or motive or the direction of the behavior, but rather upon its intrinsic characteristics. Thus, feedback may be simple or complex, positive or negative, reinforcing or not. Yet, as a consequence of behavior, feedback is closely related to the concept of reinforcement and becomes an extension to the intermediate level of this fundamental learning principle. Feedback also may or may not denote correctness, either of individual behaviors or of overall progress: for example, negative feedback does not necessarily denote that the learner has made an error, but it may serve to modify his behavior in the desired direction, while positive feedback may serve the opposite role.

Additional intermediate principles similar to those of feedback might also be cited and invented in relation to other more fundamental principles of learning. As a strategic matter, we may expect great payoff and, in my opinion, greater rewards from the development of such intermediate principles.

Now, if we agree that such intermediate principles could be worked out, how might we begin? The development of experimental laboratory schools, within school systems or separate from them, is one approach. Another, perhaps better strategically, might be the attainment of a flexible administrative structure which would permit changes in training methods from time to time or variations from class to class, along with flexible teacher and student assignments.

Within such a flexible structure, we might expect to explore possible overlaps and interactions of teacher and pupil characteristics with methods variables and then to develop definitions of methods of teaching and training independently of teachers or trainers. The most important element of this strategy is to set about developing and exploring hypotheses about the relations between the principles of learning and the principles of education, to permit greater liaison between the laboratory and the classroom. Rather than to bring the classroom to the laboratory or the laboratory to classroom, we would meet on common ground—common to both, but exclusive to neither. I cannot help but feel that by doing so, we would advance both fundamental theory and practical education.

Learning and Human Ability:
A Theoretical Approach

George A. Ferguson

McGill University

[Noting that human learning and human ability have generally each been studied by different people and by different methods, Ferguson undertakes to interrelate the two methods and to consider them jointly. He sets forth his hypotheses with clarity, and obviously considers them subject to test, revision, and verification. The important concept of transfer of training occupies a prominent place in Ferguson's system. He recommends the method of factor analysis for coping with the complexities that arise when one begins to study that area. As noted by Ferguson, this statistical approach is in essence a method designed to handle complexities and reduce them to forms that are subject to human understanding. It is usually associated with studies of human ability rather than of human learning. The comments on Ferguson's paper by Lloyd Humphreys add to the thoughts expressed by Ferguson. While not in complete accord on all counts, Humphreys tends to extend and to build on the original concepts in a constructive manner.]

Two major methodological approaches have emerged in psychology. One is experimental psychology, the other correlational psychology. Cronbach (1957) discussed the distinction in his presidential address to the American Psychological Association, *The Two Disciplines of Scientific Psychology.*

As a major field of application of the experimental method, learning has a central role in psychology. Traditionally, investigators of learning have shown little interest in correlational methods, the applications of which are best exemplified in the study of human ability. One possible approach leading to the development of a more integrated body of psychological knowledge may lie in the discovery of relationships between learning and human ability. A consideration of these two fields permits the drawing of certain comparisons.

An important point of difference resides in the role of theory. The field of learning abounds in theories of behavior. New theoretical ideas are introduced more quickly than old theoretical ideas are rejected. We have seen the emergence of theories stated in mathematical terms, as in the work of Estes (1950) and Bush and Mosteller (1955), and the revival of theories stated in neurophysiological terms, particularly in the work of Hebb (1949). In contrast to the proliferation of theories in the field of learning, those interested in the study of human ability, employing correlational methods, have evolved little systematic behavior theory. Guilford's (1956) attempt to develop a conceptual framework for mental abilities, and some of the applications of Guttman's (1957) radex model seem to be in the direction of theory. At present, however, an attempt to evaluate these approaches in relation to a more general behavior theory is probably premature. The approach of the student of human ability has been largely empirical and methodological.

Elaborate methodologies have been infrequently used to assist the construction of theories of behavior or to test the deductive consequences of such theories. This state of affairs is in marked contrast to that which prevailed in the early years of factor analysis. The early factorists, Spearman and Thompson, were interested primarily in the use of factor analysis as a theory-testing methodology. Both espoused neurophysiological theories of a rather primitive type and believed that factor analysis could be used in testing them. They disagreed not so much about method as about the inferences to be drawn from method. Certainly Spearman's book, *The Abilities of Man* (1927), is primarily concerned with theories of behavior and perhaps only secondarily with the methods of factor analysis. This theoretical orientation has in large measure disappeared among psychologists of correlational persuasion.

We are concerned here with possible applications of correlation methodology in the field of learning. Various approaches may be adopted. One is to consider direct applications of correlation methods to possible learning problems. This implies that a number of central and persisting problems in learning can be stated, and that we can assess the appropriateness of correlation methods to these problems. While this approach may prove profitable, we observe that problems selected as central in the field of learning, and their mode of formulation, are not independent of methodology. A learning theorist, on being asked to name the major problems in his field of enquiry, would probably list problems for the most part not amenable to exploration by correlation methods. An investigator in the human ability field, on being asked to list problems in the field of learning amenable to investigation by the methods familiar to him, would perhaps for the most part list problems of limited interest to the learning theorist. For example, in the definition of the stimulus or learning task, no very systematic methodology has been evolved and used by the learning theorists for describing particular learning tasks or showing how one task differs from another. The investigator usually makes decisions of this kind by inspection. Consider the field of perceptual learning. Implicit in many experiments in this field is the idea that perceptual learning may differ in important respects from other types of learning. Learning tasks are selected in conformity with vague notions about perception held by the investigator. In a perceptual learning experiment an important initial step would seem to be the definition of the learning task. At present the only method available for the description of perceptual tasks resides in Thurstone's (1944) system of perceptual factors. To the best of my knowledge no use has been made of this descriptive system in perceptual learning experiments. To date the learning theorists have shown little interest in the use of factorial methods to describe learning tasks, although to the student of human ability this might seem to be an important approach.

Another, and indirect, way to relate correlational methods to learning is at the level of theory. The relating of disparate areas of data and method by the development of more general theory is a frequently recurring feature of scientific work. In the present context this requires the development of theoretical ideas, however rudimentary, linking learning and human ability. A presumption here is that theoretical ideas linking these two fields may generate new applications of factor analysis and related correlation methods—applications of interest in both fields. My own interest has been at the level of theory, rather than in the attempt to apply factorial methods directly to existing problems in learning. The theoretical ideas I have developed have been outlined in a paper titled *Learning and Human Ability* (Ferguson, 1954). A few additional ideas were added in a subsequent paper on transfer (Ferguson, 1956). In the remainder of the present paper I shall draw upon the thoughts contained in these papers. In particular I propose to discuss the concept of ability, the nature of transfer, and a two-process theory of learning.

THE ABILITY CONCEPT

In the study of the behavior of individuals in repetitive tasks two broad classes of behavior may be identified: a class which in some crude sense is invariant with respect to repetition or its cessation and a class which is not invariant. The performance of individuals on certain tasks may exhibit considerable stability over lengthy periods of time, with little change observed either in the presence or in the absence of repetition. For convenience let us call this *invariant* behavior.

Performance on other tasks may exhibit gross improvement with repetition or gross impairment following a time interval in which no repetitions occur. Call this, for convenience, *variant* behavior. In tasks of this latter type continued repetition usually leads to invariance. A roughly asymptotic performance level or limit is reached. The terms asymptote and limit are used here only in a general way. The term plateau may perhaps be more appropriate. Further repetitions are not accompanied by improvement in performance. Repetition of a task at this asymptotic level is spoken of as overlearning. At the same time impairment in performance following a time interval in which no repetitions occur decreases with increase in the amount of overlearning. Thus variant behavior becomes invariant with repetition of a task.

Consider now the term ability. Operationally, in common usage the term refers to a measure of performance in a defined task situation. The term has ordinarily been applied to performance measures which, at least in the adult, were thought to exhibit some reasonable degree of stability over fairly lengthy periods of time. Of course, operationally the term ability can be used to refer to any performance measure. Thus learning is change in ability associated with repetition. However, in common usage, and at the operational level, the term ability in the adult has been used to refer to invariant rather than to variant performance.

These obvious and simple considerations lead us to an initial hypothesis. This hypothesis states that the abilities of the adult individual are attributes of behavior which through overlearning have reached an asymptotic level and have, thereby, attained a crude stability or invariance. This is regarded as applying to the abilities in the Thurstone classificatory system, to reasoning, number, spatial, and perceptual abilities, to whatever is assumed under intelligence as defined by conventional tests, to motor abilities, and so on. This hypothesis assigns to learning a central role in ability formation.

The above discussion is anchored in observables. Abilities are defined in terms of performance measures or functions of performance measures. We require, however, theoretical or postulational terms which are linked by inference to, or are correlated with, observables. How shall the term ability be conceptualized in theoretical terms? Here it seems appropriate to regard an ability as an intervening variable, somewhat analogous to, but in certain respects different from, Hull's habit strength variable. In Hull's theory, habit strength, "the tendency for a stimulus trace to evoke an associated response," increases as a positive growth function of the number of reinforced trials. The curve is a curve of decreasing gains, approaching a limit as the number of trials increases. The concept of habit strength, as used by Hull (1951), has reference to precisely defined stimulus response situations in which learning occurs.

Ability as an intervening variable differs from Hull's habit strength in at least two important ways. First, it refers to the limit or asymptote of the "tendency for a stimulus trace to evoke an associated response." It is conceptualized as a limit approached over a very large number of trials. Thus it may be said to be analogous to asymptotic habit strength. Second, ability as an intervening variable is much more general than Hull's habit strength variable. It is not specific to a precisely defined stimulus-response situation but may intervene as a variable in a great diversity of stimulus-response situations. How this comes about will be considered shortly in a discussion on transfer. This concept of ability is not unrelated to the concept of learning sets as proposed by Harlow (1949).

In summary we may state that abilities in the adult individual are analogous to intervening habit strength variables which through prolonged overlearning and transfer, have reached an asymptotic level, attaining, thereby, a crude stability or invariance, and which through transfer have become highly generalized, and act, or intervene, in a great diversity of stimulus-response situations.

The analogy between the concepts of ability and habit strength is open to question on a number of counts. Nonetheless it is possibly a useful analogy.

TRANSFER

In the adult all learning occurs within the context of prior learning. Transfer effects operate. In common usage the essence of the concept of transfer is that change in performance on task A, resulting from practice, will exert an effect on performance on task B, or on change in performance on task B. This statement of what is meant by transfer is unsatisfactory in several respects. In the 1956 paper I suggested the concept of a general transfer function and considered particular instances of that function. Elaboration of these ideas is hardly warranted here. Any commonly accepted notion of transfer will serve our present purpose.

If abilities are viewed as variables which through learning have reached a fairly stable level, these variables will produce important effects in many learning situations. Thus a problem in which ability test scores are related to performance at various levels of practice, or to measures of change in performance at various levels of practice, may be conceptualized as a problem in transfer. In somewhat different terms, the abilities, viewed as intervening variables, may act in many stimulus-response situations. They mediate the response. Further, it may be argued that the most important intervening variables acting in most stimulus-response situations are the abilities. Although not explicitly formulated, this idea has frequently been accepted implicitly by educationists.

Let us now consider the way in which abilities affect learning. Here a postulate of differential transfer may be stated. This postulate of differential transfer states that in many learning tasks abilities exert their effects differentially. The abilities which transfer and produce their effects at one stage of learning may differ from those which transfer and produce their effects at other stages of learning. Thus the abilities as intervening variables act differentially in a stimulus-response situation as a function of the number of trials.

A consequence of this postulate is that individual differences in abilities, which may be related to individual differences in performance in the early stages of learning a task, may not be related, or may be related in a different way, to performance at some later stage of learning. Thus an individual may have the abilities necessary to perform a task at a high level of proficiency, but may lack the ability to learn to perform the task under particular conditions of learning. Conversely an individual may have the abilities necessary for rapid improvement in the early stages of learning a task, but may lack the abilities necessary for an ultimate high level of proficiency.

The work of Fleishman and Hempel (1954, 1955) on psychomotor learning provides substantial evidence in support of the concept of differential transfer. The implications of the concept for selection and training are considerable.

A consideration of the effects of abilities on learning must provide for both positive and negative transfer. Prior learning may not only facilitate but may inhibit subsequent learning. It is not entirely improbable that in the learning of certain tasks different abilities may exert positive and negative effects simultaneously, one ability facilitating and another inhibiting performance. Further, an ability may exert a facilitating effect at one stage and an inhibitory effect at a later stage. Any theory concerned with the effects of prior learning on subsequent learning must provide for the possibility both of positive and negative effects.

A TWO-PROCESS THEORY OF LEARNING

A number of theorists, including Hebb (1949), have emphasized a difference between early and late learning, that is between learning in childhood and learning in the adult. The idea here is that early learning is a process whereby certain basic elements are built up. In Hebb's theory these elements are assigned neurophysiological meaning. Adult learning, on the other hand, is considered a process whereby basic elements are organized or reorganized in new arrangements. Thus learning in the adult results largely from transfer.

Some form of two-process theory of learning appears to be necessary, because any attempt to explain all learning in terms of transfer obviously cannot explain how early learning can occur at all.

A two-process theory of learning may be stated in the following terms. All learning, excluding some very early learning, involves not only transfer components but also components which are specific to the new learning task. In the language of factor analysis this means that variation in performance at various stages of learning a task can be accounted for in part by the abilities developed through prior learning and in part by abilities that are formed during the process of learning the task itself. Thus factors specific to the learning task may emerge. This theory bears a certain analogic relation to Spearman's two-factor theory. In Spearman's theory performance on a task was conceptualized as involving general and specific components. In the present theory performance at various stages of learning a task is conceptualized as involving a set of general ability variables and one or more variables specific to the particular learning task. Fleishman's studies on psychomotor learning in adult subjects suggest the formation of within-task abilities. If this is so, and the evidence is anything but conclusive, one implication is that the prediction of human behavior may always exhibit some degree of unpredictability or indeterminancy.

A two-process theory of learning is required to account both for the correlation between abilities and for their differentiation. Those abilities will tend to develop which are facilitated and not inhibited by one another. General and common factors result from positive transfer. An explanation of the fact that abilities, although in many instances correlated, are clearly differentiated one from another seems to require the postulation of a second process leading to within-task factors.

While differences in early learning and later learning may perhaps in some measure be understood in terms of the relative importance of transfer in relation to other processes, such an approach should not overlook the role of negative transfer. Certain things are learned more readily by the adult, other things more readily by the child. T¹ e introduction of negative transfer as an explanatory principle may account for some of these differences. Thus, in second language learning in the adult it seems probable that negative transfer effects may operate in the early stages of the acquisition of the second language, whereas in the child at a certain age such negative effects do not operate, or do not operate to the same extent, and the second language is more readily acquired. If this idea can be shown by experiment to have substance, it bears on the long standing question of the most advantageous time to introduce the child to a second language. Presumably second language learning should be introduced at a stage which takes advantage of the positive effects of prior learning and avoids the negative effects, if such a stage can be determined.

This is a brief summary of certain aspects of the theoretical ideas I have attempted to develop. Other aspects of these theoretical ideas have been discussed elsewhere (Ferguson, 1954). In my opinion, these ideas establish certain relations between the fields of human learning and human ability and lead to the formulation of problems amenable to exploration by factor analytic and related methods. These problems are largely in the field of transfer of training. It seems to me that factor analysis may serve as a methodology which will permit the investigation of problems which are closer to learning as it actually occurs in the child and in the adult, and may assist the development of behavior theories of a generality greater than some of the existing ones. As we all know, much contemporary learning theory is concerned exclusively with the behavior of rats or humans in highly contrived situations, and is of low generality. Factor analysis may have much to contribute to the development of more general behavior theory, because, despite its limitations, it is in essence a method for handling complexity. Everything we know about human behavior suggests that any method which can reduce aspects of highly complex phenomena to forms receptive to our understanding may have something to contribute.

Discussion of Ferguson's Paper

Lloyd G. Humphreys

George Ferguson has convinced us that he is too modest. He has good ideas, and even some data which at the beginning he denied having. However, I would like to quibble with the terminology he used in his introductory paragraphs. I do not like his distinction between experimental and correlational methods. There is a better way of talking about the difference, which is a real one. I prefer to say that all science involves correlation. In some areas the independent variable is under the control of the experimentalist. In other investigations it is not. One set of correlations are those which are determined experimentally; the second are correlations between variables as one finds them. The latter might be called ad hoc correlations. In that regard, I find it useful at times to transform t-ratios into point bi-serial correlation coefficients. When an experimentalist friend gets excited by a highly significant t-ratio, it may turn out to be equivalent to a .20 correlation coefficient. I think the transformation has a salutory effect. Perhaps it would be helpful if we talked more frequently about all types of research as correlational research and actually translated results from one context to the other.

My next point concerns the difference between Ferguson's direct and indirect applications. Quite correctly he passes over the direct application of research methodology to experimental psychology. However, I want to point out that these problems, even though he has gone over them lightly, are nevertheless exceedingly important. I refer, of course, to the use of our methodology for classifying independent and dependent variables. Benton Underwood, in his recent book, pays a good deal of attention to the problem of the classification of variables in experimental psychology. It is an important problem that experimentalists have largely neglected. One gets an idea, seizes upon a situation which is thought to be appropriate, and adopts as the dependent variable that which is easiest to measure in this situation, without regard to other important considerations. The time is ripe to get away from this approach to the careful selection of independent and dependent variables in experimental work.

The indirect applications are the heart of Ferguson's paper. One of the concepts he mentions is the difference between variant and invariant behavior. I would like to add to the discussion of these terms. In the first place, we both recognize that these form a continuum, but there is still some confusion concerning the application of the term invariance to psychological data. Really it has two quite different meanings.

Many think of invariance as the place on the learning curve where group means no longer change. Now, it is quite possible for a group to have reached a plateau where additional stimulation will not increase group performance. However, within the group the correlation between adjacent trials may still show a gradual change. This can come about if individual learning curves have not reached stable plateaus. The group plateau can be relatively stable and yet the individual learning curves may not have achieved stability. This will produce the change in function as indicated by the correlation between adjacent trials.

Even though the group curve achieves stability, some individual curves may go down when others go up, so that they compensate. Recently I looked at some data on the pecking behavior of pigeons illustrating this point nicely. It has been said that it is easy to get pigeons or rats up to a stable plateau and that when they reach this stable level of performance you can do various things experimentally with them with the stable base line as the control. However, Schoenfeld asked just how stable stable is. How much change is there in the individual pigeon's performance over an extended period of time? I believe he ran his pigeons for something like 220 days. The group curves were quite stable during this period, but the individual pigeon pecking response would proceed along a plateau for a number of days, then go up or down. The variability of individual curves was about 25 per cent of the individual pigeon's means over the entire period of 220 days. With group means remaining fairly steady, and with individual pigeons behaving in this fashion, it is quite clear that these data would generate the kind of correlational matrices that we have been discussing. The explanations for these changes in the performance of the pigeons are hard to determine. The pigeons were kept in a relatively constant state, but it is possible that there were internal physiological changes which would account for some of these changes in performance level.

I find the equations that Ferguson makes between ability and habit strength and learning set to be quite acceptable, and even intriguing. It is one to which we need to pay attention. As he points out, the relationship between Harlow's learning set concept and ability is probably a good deal closer than that of Hull's habit strength to ability.

In discussing the relations between ability and transfer I would like to suggest some possible experimental manipulations which I think may supplement what has been said. The transfer situation is commonly presented as follows:

Group I: Pretest$_1$—Transfer Training—Posttest$_1$

Group II: Pretest$_1$—Inactivity—Posttest$_1$

One does not, of course, necessarily need the pretest but it is a nice additional control. In Group II we have a pretest, then inactivity or a meaningless activity such as color naming, and finally the posttest. In Group I the interpolated activity is utilized as a means of promoting transfer. The amount of transfer is measured by the difference between the two posttests, assuming that the pretest means are comparable. Now, we may add a second variable.

Group I: Pretest$_1$—Transfer Training—Posttest$_1$
Pretest$_2$ Posttest$_2$

Group II: Pretest$_1$—Inactivity—Posttest$_1$
Pretest$_2$ Posttest$_2$

We can measure the amount of transfer to Test 1 by computing the difference between Posttest$_1$ for Groups I and II. We can measure the amount of transfer to Test 2 by computing the difference between Posttest$_2$ for Groups I and II.

Before training, let Test 1 and Test 2 be orthogonal. Assuming that the special training produces transfer for both Tests 1 and 2, if we compute the correlation between 1 and 2 over both groups, 1 and 2 will now be positively correlated. The amount of correlation will be a function of the change in the means produced by the special training. We would ordinarily call this a spurious correlation, I suppose. It is a correlation due to the means. The within groups correlation is still zero but there is now an over-all correlation between these tests where previously we had no correlation.

Now, let us put in Tests 1, 2, 3 . . . m. This produces an extension of the same phenomenon, that is, the level of intercorrelations of these m posttests will depend upon the amount of transfer arising from the special training. If no transfer results for, say, test $(m - 1)$ it will be uncorrelated with the other variables. If only a little transfer results, one will find small correlations with some of the other variables, and so on.

Now, let us add to this picture by introducing n variations of the independent variable. Again any correlations produced will be a function of the means. These variations of the independent variable do not have to be along a single continuum because with respect to plotting the correlation for the group as a whole we simply, in effect, use as the continuum the size of the difference produced by the various experimental treatments. If treatment X produces the largest amount of transfer for these variables consistently, then this group will in effect have its scores in the top of the score distribution.

Let us now make one other assumption, namely, that in place of doing this in a laboratory, we assume that this takes place in life in the home, in the school, or on the playground. In this instance I think we will have generated the intercorrelations among tests that Ferguson has talked about.

Suppose we give direct training on Test 2 and find that this training does not transfer to Test 1 with which Test 2 is correlated. It is at least possible that both tests have elements in common with the previous background training events, which produced the correlation between the tests, but do not have elements in common with each other required for transfer from one to the other. In other words, we cannot necessarily expect transfer between correlated posttest measures, even though the correlation between them has been produced by transfer in the way Ferguson has described.

We were somewhat surprised during World War II to find that the two-hand coordination test showed the biggest difference between the Chinese and the American cadet groups. It is difficult for me to believe that this indicates a biological difference between the Chinese and Americans. Rather it looks like a cultural phenomenon arising out of real-life training situations. American children have considerable experience with wheeled toys, carpentry tools and even the specialized lathes which the two-handed coordination tests most closely resemble. Among American boys the whole gamut of early experiences builds up an ability to do well in such things as the two-handed coordination test. Among Chinese boys early experiences led perhaps to other skills.

In general the Chinese male profiles follow very closely the American female profile on the World War II aircrew tests. As you might expect, the test that produced the next largest difference was our version of the Bennett Mechanical Comprehension Test. In turn, one finds that the two-handed coordination test is substantially correlated with the Bennett Mechanical Comprehension Test.

With respect to Ferguson's two-factor theory, it seems to me that with a generalized transfer function you do not really need the two factors. Thompson's theory of overlapping elements is perhaps closer to what Ferguson is getting at than is Spearman's theory.

Finally, I would like to suggest that the place in which we ought perhaps to look for biological determination of abilities as opposed to a learning transfer explanation is in someway akin to Spearman's g-factor. If we were to take the primary mental abilities delineated by Thurstone, or even as they have been expanded by others, and score these ipsatively we might find that the ipsative profile is largely or entirely determined by transfer variance. The place to look for biological factors may be in the height of the profile removed by the ipsative scoring.

Further Discussion of Ferguson's Paper

Marion E. Bunch

I would like to comment on some aspects of transfer of training as it applies to learning.

Laboratory studies indicate that in virtually all instances of transfer of training from one problem, A, to another similar problem, B, both positive and negative transfer effects are present. Let us suppose that one group (control) of college students learns problem B in 120 trials and a comparable group (transfer), which had previously learned problem A, required only 100 trials to learn problem B. We would then state that the transfer effect was positive in character—a saving of 20 trials— but by no means ought we to imply that no negative transfer effect occurred. Negative transfer may have occurred in the early trials on problem B, but may have been overshadowed by the positive effect. The final result in terms of total scores may be the algebraic sum of the factors which tend to retard and those which tend to facilitate the later learning of B.

In the study of cumulative transfer varying numbers of similar problems are learned prior to problem B and their respective transfer effect determined. In representing graphically the learning of a single task, the points on the abscissa customarily represent successive trials on the problem, but in representing graphically the effects of cumulative transfer the successive points on the abscissa usually represent the previous problems learned and the order in which they are learned.

Of course, it may be that in the learning curve of a single problem we are also representing transfer of training in which the successive trials are smaller blocks of learning than would be involved in a number of successive problems of a similar nature. Thus, in some studies of cumulative transfer only a few problems have been used. However, in Harlow's work on learning to learn, 350 or more tasks were used in which each particular task involved only a limited number of trials. The same principles which determine cumulative transfer effects from previous problems may also be determining the cumulative effects from successive trials in a single task.

In addition, I would like to note that the ability to utilize the learning from a prior task in solving a new problem may be markedly different from merely the retention of the prior problem, and may have a different course through time from that of forgetting. When the subject comes to learn problem B later, a certain amount of A must obviously have been retained or there will be no carryover from the earlier learning. Similarly, in a single task the only reason the subject is better off on the twentieth trial than on the first is that he retains and transfers the effects of the first 19 trials. In the single task it may be that the two important factors determining improvement are transfer and retention, that is, how much is retained and how much is transferred from one trial to the next during learning. Furthermore, individual differences in learning may largely be a function of the difference between these individuals in the extent to which they remember the effects of earlier trials and their ability to carry over and utilize the effects from the earlier trials. Several laboratory studies indicate that the temporal course of transfer is, under some conditions, significantly different from that of forgetting and that in some instances it seems to function despite a considerable amount of forgetting.

I am much more concerned with measuring this kind of improvement than with trying to predict final status from initial status. It may well be that one can predict final status better from other information than from initial status. But I think in laboratory studies of learning, the essential characteristics with regard to which we are trying to get the most precise measure possible is the improvement that does take place between initial and final status. I think that this is the more important single factor with regard to the measurement of learning. If the statistical or correlational approach can be combined with the laboratory approach, more conditions can be controlled than in either approach alone and more accurate measures be made of the improvement in learning.

It has been stated that by correlational procedures alone one might be able to determine by simplex structure what is the best order in which a series of tasks should be learned. This is a way in which laboratory studies can profit from the correlational approach. Predictions made in advance can be checked empirically. Some studies made in learning indicate, for example, that even when two similar tasks appear equal in difficulty, the transfer effect may be a function of the order in which they are learned. If they are unequal in difficulty, the transfer effect may be greater from the easy to the more difficult than when they are learned in the reverse order.

A measure of learning that would be more desirable and useful than many currently used in laboratory studies would be one structured in terms of the increases in the probability of the occurrence of the correct acts as a function of practice. I think we need to measure improvement in terms of increments of probability of the correct response occurring in succeeding practice trials rather than in terms of errors, repetitions, or response latency for example, although these methods may be vastly superior to trials-to-extinction as a measure of learning.

Insights on Methods of Training Research
From Laboratory Studies of Learning

Marion E. Bunch

Washington University

[The sheer volume and complexity of research on learning poses a major problem for the individual engaged in practical educational pursuits. It should be possible for someone who has an extensive knowledge of the research literature and is conversant with practical training situations to select from the literature those concepts, findings, and applications that are most pertinent to the typical training situation. It would be difficult to find an individual better qualified to perform this important service than Marion Bunch. Centering his remarks around the topics of stimulus generalization, experimental extinction, transfer of training, interference in learning, and reminiscence, Bunch summarizes what is known about these phenomena and how it applies to the practical training situation. He also points to what is not known, and hence to important research areas. No one should accept the often repeated statement that laboratory-derived information has nothing to offer in a practical training situation without first giving consideration to Bunch's thought-provoking paper.

However, in the discussion which follows the paper, it becomes quite clear that not all training researchers feel that the insights from the laboratory related by Bunch can be generalized to practical training situations. This position is developed in an interesting and provocative manner by Wilse B. Webb. Eventually, Bunch and Webb arrive at common ground in the view that the laboratory provides broad, general principles; numerical relationships associated with these principles vary from one situation to another and are not, or at least should not be, claimed as general.]

Among the basic characteristics of learning important in determining whether some training methods are better than others are: *stimulus generalization, experimental extinction, transfer of training, interference in learning,* and *reminiscence.* I shall single out the major features of each and show how they are pertinent to determining efficiency of learning.

STIMULUS GENERALIZATION AND EXTINCTION

When we are trying to associate a particular stimulus with a particular response, we find that the tendency of this stimulus to call forth the response increases from the beginning of training. Once learning begins there is a tendency for the response to generalize to other stimuli similar to the stimulus used in training. Consider a tone of 256 c.p.s. as a stimulus. By proper training it becomes associated with a given response. We then discover that similar frequencies will now arouse the response. These stimuli, however, were not used in training. The only one used in training was the critical one of 256 c.p.s. The response thereafter is nevertheless made to other stimuli. This generalization undoubtedly begins with the *onset* of learning. The question is: what is the shape of the curve of this generalization tendency? How does stimulus generalization develop during the process of learning? Presumably we have an orderly, progressive development of changes which begins with the very first trial. As training continues, the probability that this stimulus will call forth the response increases, and we can represent the increase on the vertical coordinate in Figure 1. The probability that other stimuli, similar but different quantitatively, will arouse the same response also increases. The shape of the gradient is not definitely known. Of several suggestions in the literature, the one represented in Figure 1 is probably the best known.

If we continue the training still further, we raise the level of the curve above the base line. We increase not only the tendency to respond to the stimulus used in training but also the likelihood that other stimuli will call forth the same response. While the curve in Figure 1 is often presented because of the advantages it gives in a theoretical controversy, it is not confirmed by the experimental data. Another individual, in the same school of learning theory, has suggested that the curve is probably negatively accelerated. This view has not been used much, probably because it does not fit the outlines of the controversy.

Actually, stimulus generalization must be considered along with experimental extinction. If we want to establish discrimination between two similar stimuli so that the subject makes the response to S_1 but

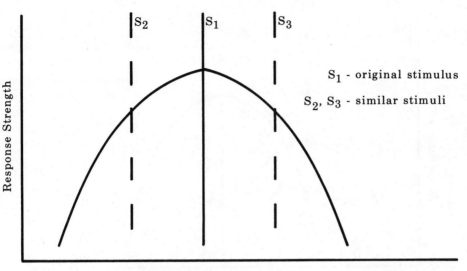

S_1 - original stimulus

S_2, S_3 - similar stimuli

Figure 1. Stimulus Generalization Curve

never to S_2, we may proceed in accordance with the principle of differential reinforcement. Continued reinforcement will maintain the response to S_1 while failure to reinforce the generalized response to S_2 will result in its extinction. This extinction process is cumulative, and at a particular stage of training may generalize to similar stimuli in the manner shown in Figure 2.

As the extinction procedure continues, extinction increases, the gradient probably changes in shape, and finally we may have the situation in which sharp discrimination has been achieved. As shown in Figure 3, the response is now generalized only to a very narrow range of stimuli around S_1 and the tendency to make the response to stimuli outside this narrow band has suffered extinction.

Presumably, all during the course of learning, in discriminating between the two stimuli, we have the two functions interacting with each other. The progressive changes in the shape of the gradients are not known. At the end of training, when the subject has mastered the task, he now makes this response only to the correct stimulus; it is no longer made to any of the others that are used by the experimenter. It may be that as the curve gets higher and higher, the generalized response becomes more and more restricted until finally it is shown to a very narrow band of similar stimuli; how narrow depends perhaps upon the extent of overtraining.

These processes may go on in almost any discrimination learning the person undertakes. What is needed is information concerning the de-

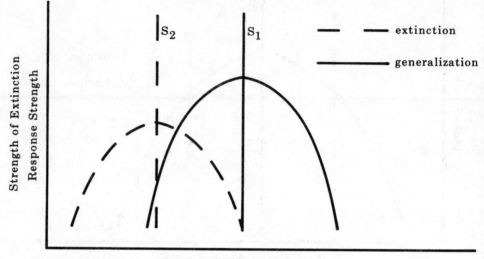

Figure 2. Curves of Generalization and Extinction

velopment of these generalization curves, from the initial point where learning begins, through the point of mastery, to some degree of over-learning. The exact shape of the generalization gradient at an early stage of training and the progressive gradient changes with continued training for the material or components being learned in a particular problem, are questions of considerable practical as well as theoretical

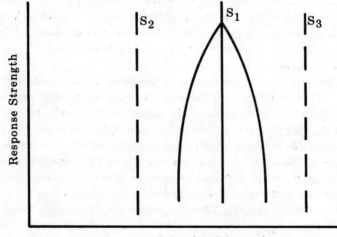

Figure 3. Stimulus Generalization Curve Following Discrimination Learning

significance. Similarly we need information with regard to the process of extinguishing the generalized conditioned responses.

Information concerning these gradients during learning should be of aid in advancing our understanding of many practical problems in learning on which the evidence appears contradictory. For example, suppose we look at the question of whether or not learners who are rapid in learning retain longer or better than slow learners. The answer to this question might have considerable usefulness in training programs. As you may know we have inconsistent results on this question, despite the fact that it was first attacked experimentally more than 60 years ago. Several experimental procedures have been used in studying the relationship. One method was suggested on the basis of the argument that, since the slow learner will obviously take more time or trials to learn the task and since not all items in the task will be of equal difficulty, the slow learner may be expected to overlearn the easy items while taking the larger number of trials to master the items which are difficult for him. Later, as a result of overlearning the easy items, the slow learner may be expected to show better retention for the problem as a whole. The way to combat this, it was thought, was to withdraw individual items from the list as soon as they were mastered. That is, a criterion of learning such as one perfect trial, which is usually applied to the problem as a whole, should be applied to the individual items being memorized. But one might note in criticism that withdrawing items from the list being memorized may change the problem so greatly as to make it questionable whether the slow and fast learners are then learning the same problem. Two functions presumably are developing during the learning: one is the correct response to each stimulus and the generalization of this response to other similar stimuli, and the other is the extinction of wrong generalized responses. When we take items away from the list during learning, we no longer are dealing with the same order of difficulty and opportunities for interaction among all parts of the problem. We may have changed the list to such a degree that it becomes a different and somewhat easier problem for the learner, and the experimenter is unable even to estimate the extent to which the task has been reduced in complexity. Evidence relevant to this point may be noted when we double the length of a task: the task may be more than doubled in difficulty in terms of the time required to master it. This is thought to be the result largely of the disproportionate increase in interference that presumably occurs between the various component parts of the problem. We need more information concerning the progressive changes in the gradients of generalization for the primary stimulus items during learning and similar information on the strength of the generalized extinction tendencies for instances in which the subject is likely to make erroneous responses because of the similarity of stimuli. Until this information becomes available, the method noted above for studying the relative retentive abilities of fast and slow learners may remain suspect.

There is evidence, however, which suggests that this conception may be premature, because extinction may not be an unlearning function as is often assumed.

STIMULUS GENERALIZATION AS A FUNCTION OF TIME

So far as I can find out an important aspect of generalization has not been studied at all. Yet this factor must be involved in all training involving fairly complex learning. The question is: how do generalization tendencies vary with the passage of time? Suppose we had information showing the generalization gradient at the moment we stop learning. Then we allow time to pass and have a separate group for each of the time intervals which we wish to study. The question is: what happens to this particular function of generalization during short intervals of time? Is the generalization gradient a function of time similar to that in reminiscence or in transfer of training? I know of no evidence on this matter. From the standpoint of efficiency of learning, the problem of the time relationship would seem to be as important here as in forgetting. We have a very large number of studies with respect to forgetting, tending to show the usual curve of how material learned decreases in habit strength or performance with passage of time. We have no such information concerning generalization. Yet this would be important from the standpoint of predicting how an individual will function after a period of time. In the practical situation, we may regard all learning as preparation for future contingencies. We learn a skill with the idea of using it at some future date. Information concerning the course of generalization through time would seem to be extremely pertinent. As is well known, introducing a time interval during the process of learning frequently is followed by improvement in learning. We have an amazing amount of evidence on this matter. It may be that introducing a time interval during learning is important because of what happens to the stimulus generalization gradient during the interval. It is surprising that we do not have evidence of experimental recognition of the importance of this question.

THE TIME INTERVAL AND TRANSFER
FROM ONE LEARNING SITUATION TO ANOTHER

Let us now discuss learning in the context of the influence of one task upon another similar one. Here is where generalization and transfer of training come together. We have evidence that, if the person learns a given problem, A, then waits a period of time to learn problem B, and the transfer of training that occurs from A to B under these circumstances is compared with that which occurs when A and B are learned in immediate succession, the results indicate a particular trend, though not always a consistent one. Surprisingly enough, more often than not the transfer of training from A to B does not change with the time interval. We do not have the generalizable information we need in order to carry over conclusions to practical situations in training. Under some conditions we have a curve that looks almost like a reminiscence curve. The extent to which training on one task is utilized in the learning of a similar problem later is to some extent a function of the time interval. The interval used in studies which found the amount of transfer to be independent of time has been as long as 120 days. Compared with many studies on memory and transfer, this is a fairly long interval. But if one were to allow a much longer interval, the function would undoubtedly drop as the amount retained became minimal.

REMINISCENCE, ECONOMY OF DISTRIBUTED PRACTICE, AND AGE

Another factor with regard to short intervals of time is that of reminiscence, which would seem to be a basic factor in learning. If individuals master a task to what is customarily regarded as complete mastery, or 100 per cent learning, and retention is measured after varying intervals of time, we usually present a retention curve as shown in Figure 4. When learning is stopped at some point in initial training below complete mastery—at only 75 per cent mastery, or 50 per cent, or at any arbitrarily selected level—we do not get a retention curve that parallels

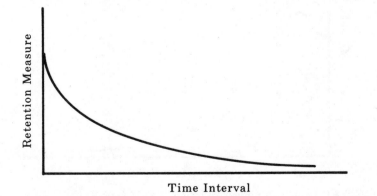

Figure 4. Retention as a Function of Time

that found in the retention of completely learned material. What is often found is a curve that at first rises and subsequently drops as shown in Figure 5.

In the retention test after a short period of time the subject recalls more than he was able to recall immediately upon cessation of practice. If we use methods other than recall, we still get this phenomenon. It is found for verbal material, for motor tasks, for older subjects as well as the younger ones. It is found for dull children, for bright children, and has been noted in the retention curve of rats in a maze problem. It would seem to be a rather general and basic characteristic of the temporal course of incomplete learning for a wide variety of materials.

One suggestion as to why this occurs is that reminiscence depends upon reactive inhibition. Each time the subject performs the response, there is set up a negative tendency toward doing it again. This may be thought of as similar to, but not identical with, fatigue. Like fatigue, it presumably would increase with the number of times the act is performed. It is greater after many performances than after one or two. It disappears with time. As it disappears, whatever inhibiting effect it had upon learning presumably disappears as well. Reactive inhibition is often mentioned as one of the factors that may influence reminiscence. It may also be important in accounting for the economy of distributed practice. It is as if limited practice produces a rise in the learning curve, and then, when we introduce a rest interval, the curve rises without requiring practice. Practice periods are alternated with rest periods until mastery. Learning is often more economical if we take advantage of the increments that occur during rest periods. Distributed practice may really depend upon the phenomenon of reminiscence during learning.

If reminiscence depends upon reactive inhibition, then certain de-

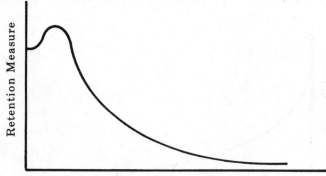

Time Interval

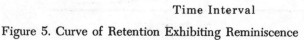

Figure 5. Curve of Retention Exhibiting Reminiscence

ductions would seem to follow logically. One is that this function would vary with the ages of the subjects. Most of the studies have indicated that reminiscence is very great in young children up to 12 years of age. In fact 12 is often the age at which reminiscence for the same kind of material is found to be most pronounced. It has been found sometimes in individuals around 20, and occasionally in some older than 20. It probably occurs at all ages. One recent study found that the relationship between reminiscence and age was of the order shown in Figure 6, in which reminiscence increased with age up to the early 20's, and then declined. The first impression in looking at the curve is that this is a curve representing the relationship between age and learning ability. Reminiscence did not reach its peak in individuals around 12, but increased into the 20's and seemed to be very pronounced clear into the 60's. While the oldest subjects used were around 70, the average of the older group was in the low 60's.

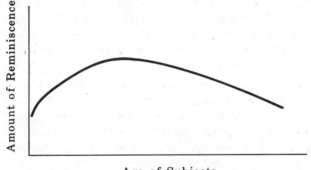

Figure 6. Reminiscence as a Function of Age

Now if reminiscence is a function of reactive inhibition and is similar in this respect to fatigue, one might think that the process would be greater in older individuals. Performing the act the same number of times would be expected to set up more reactive inhibition for the 60-year old than it would in the young person. In turn, a short interval of time should be more beneficial to the older individual. So reactive inhibition may not be the important factor underlying reminiscence after all. At least, it does not seem to vary with age exactly in the way that would be expected.

Another point is related. When the experimenter subdivided his group with regard to mental age and selected groups of the same mental age but of different chronological ages, practically no relationship was found between increasing chronological age and reminiscence.

Thus, reminiscence increased with chronological age largely because mental age was also increasing, so that the results indicate that the amount of reminiscence is largely a function of mental age. This finding fails to fit in with the view that reminiscence is a function of the effort in performing an act. It is entirely consistent with the view that reminiscence may be important in determining that distributed practice during the process of learning is more effective than massed practice.

CUMULATIVE TRANSFER AND DISTRIBUTED PRACTICE ON A SINGLE COMPLEX TASK

Another set of phenomena relates to cumulative effects of transfer of training. If a person learns several tasks which are very similar one to another, transfer of training is cumulative through the successive problems, and in the main the effect is positive. When we get negative transfer in laboratory studies it is apt to be limited to the first few trials on the task. In terms of total scores it is rather difficult to get negative transfer effects. It may be that parts of task A will transfer positively and facilitate the later learning of B, while other parts of A will transfer and interfere with the later learning of B, if these are fairly complicated tasks. The positive transfer effect is generally the more pronounced and outweighs the negative effect. Of course negative transfer may occur, leading to errors in the second test. From the standpoint of safety in the practical situation the errors may be so costly that the negative transfer effect may be the all-important factor. But in terms of laboratory study, where one is not concerned with the cost of the error, and transfer is measured in total scores, positive transfer predominates. Eight problems will transfer and help the subject more in learning the ninth than four would help in learning the fifth. How far this goes is difficult to show. We can point to results which indicate that transfer may go on for hundreds of tasks. However, in some instances the successive problems may be so related to each other and to an ultimate problem which may be considered as a goal that the final solution may be analogous to the goal in a single task. Then it would appear that what we are dealing with would not really be something new in the form of transfer from earlier problems to later ones, but rather something analogous to cumulative transfer in successive trials in the learning of a single complex task.

We are thinking here of studies in which monkeys established learning sets in a series of 300 to 400 problems of the same type. Cumulative transfer is marked in instances where the rate of learning new sets depends increasingly on the learning sets previously acquired.

Some earlier studies asked if an animal could learn a concept such as that of triangularity. Is this concept something only a higher organism can learn? Almost immediately applicable to the problem is one of the basic characteristics of learning, cumulative transfer. When the researchers attempted to teach a white rat the concept of triangularity, it required hundreds of trials. They were first able to establish a generalization tendency by rewarding the rat for choosing the triangle. When the response was made to a rectangle during training, the response went unrewarded and was gradually extinguished. Now the animal had learned to go to the triangle and not to the rectangle. The experimenters could then proceed by presenting a triangle with a circle. This discrimination constituted the second task. Then through a series of tasks, the animal was trained to respond to a wide variety of triangles when presented with other forms and with control of position, area, and brightness. The final result was that the animal came to respond positively to new and different figures when they possessed the properties common to all triangles.

Thus, by learning several successive simple discrimination problems which are related to one another in a definite manner, an animal can be trained to the point where it is responding on the basis of a concept, such as of triangularity.

In cumulative transfer studies where the problems are so related to each other that there is a solution which has general applicability, the total cumulative effect may not be fully achieved until many separate problems have been learned. In other instances where the problems are not so related to each other, e.g., in successive lists of nonsense syllables where the cumulative transfer occurs mostly as the result of practice effects, the maximum amount may be reached relatively quickly. For example, in learning successive lists of nonsense syllables, the subjects were only slightly better learners of this kind of material after 16 such problems than they were after having learned five similar problems.

A related problem concerns transfer in the retention performance. The subject, after mastering similar problems, is asked to perform test A, an earlier task. We discover that the tasks learned during the interval since learning A interfere with the retention of A. The greater the number of tasks learned during the interval the greater, within limits, is the loss in the retention of A. It is, however, important to separate recall from relearning. When we ask the subject to recall task A, we are likely to find that the greater the number of similar problems he has learned during the interval, the poorer will be his recall. The effect may continue down to the level of failure to recall at all. Suppose, however, instead of asking him to recall what was learned, we ask him to relearn A. He is started on task A and continues on it until his proficiency is at the level that he had achieved at first. Here the factors of generalization, extinction, and transfer interact in relearning to give us a curve that looks somewhat like the one in Figure 7.

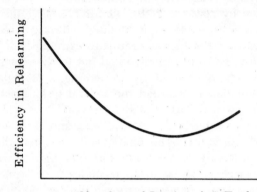

Figure 7. Transfer as a Function of the Number of Tasks Intervening between Original Learning and Relearning

If efficiency in relearning is represented on the vertical coordinate of Figure 7, and the number of similar problems learned since the first task is represented on the abscissa, the curve tends to drop for a number of problems and then rise, showing some improvement after a relatively large number of intervening problems. Strictly speaking this would seem to be definitely a transfer phenomenon though it goes under the heading of retroactive inhibition or perhaps facilitation when the curve rises. For example, suppose there are many tasks before the subject returns to the relearning of A. Retention of A is brought down to a low level, as indicated by measures of relearning. Adding similar problems in the interval may now transfer positively to the relearning of what has been forgotten of A more than it interferes with what he remembers of A at this point. It is as if the first interpolated tasks of similar problems tended to efface his memory of A. We then give him some additional similar problems and find that they help him more in relearning what has been forgotten than they interfere with the small amount he still retains. So the curve starts to rise again, showing the extreme complexity in the interaction of parts within a problem and between similar problems. We do not know the generalization curves or how they develop during continued practice or how they vary from one problem to another.

SPREAD OF EFFECT PHENOMENON

Another principle from the laboratory—the principle of the spread of effect in learning—had very doubtful status for a long time, but now it seems to be not an artifact but genuine in character.

Suppose we have a problem in which we want S_1 associated with R_1, S_2 associated with R_2, S_3 with R_3, and so on for a number of paired items. The problem may consist of foreign vocabulary words to be associated with their English equivalents. If we do not give the subject knowledge of results concerning *all* of his responses, but give him the information only on certain widely separated pairs, we are able to determine whether the effect of the knowledge is limited to the stimulus-response pair it follows. For example, knowledge that the response to S_4 is right not only strengthens this association, as indicated by the fact that the next time we present S_4 the probability that it will arouse R_4 has been increased, but it also increases the probability that other responses made to stimuli near S_4 will be repeated on the next trial. It may even increase slightly the probability that others, which were found to be wrong, will be repeated. Suppose S_3 calls forth R_3, and we tell the subject that this is wrong. Normally this would tend to weaken the association. If this S-R pair is close to another stimulus response relationship that is rewarded, it will be strengthened to some degree. The strengthening effect spreads to neighboring items but becomes less as the stimulus-response relationships become more remote. It extends usually over three or four items. Under some circumstances it has been found to extend as far as the fifth or sixth item. The effect is on both sides of the rewarded response.

These are a few of the principles and characteristics of learning which seem to me to be important in determining the efficiency of a learner in a training situation. They have been singled out in preference to some of the more traditional principles because they seem to have received little or no attention in training programs. Although these principles are based in the main on laboratory work with traditional methods and materials, they are presumably involved in many different kinds of learning. The extent to which particular characteristics of learning are a function of time would seem to be of considerable practical importance. If we had more information on these principles we would in all probability be able to make better recommendations for modifications in training procedures. One practical problem is to reduce the lag between the knowledge of principles found in the laboratory and specific information about their operation in training programs with their particular materials and circumstances.

Discussion of Bunch's Paper

Wilse B. Webb

Marion Bunch's paper reminds me somewhat of a Dorothy Parker situation. Late one night while sound asleep she had a dream that suddenly gave her all the truths of the world. She quickly reached for a pencil on her night stand and wrote down this great truth. She woke up the next morning to find she had written, "Higamos, hogamus, all women are monogamous; hogamus, higamos, all men are polygamous."

Sometimes as I look at learning results, I think that I see great truths. But when I wake up in the gray dawn of applying these truths I find great difficulty.

I remember once saying, "Let's take a typical situation of learning from the real world, such as the transfer from field to carrier landing, or from flying the aircraft in the day to flying the aircraft at night, and consider it as a simple, straightforward learning situation." But as you turn to the task itself you find that the stimuli involved amount to several hours in the air with a man on the ground frantically waving his arms and with another man, who has partially learned the task, trying to control the aircraft so it will come down safely. Trials are distributed with intervals of days and sometimes weeks. Sometimes trials occur twice in a day. Reward is intangible and is likely to differ for each man. Furthermore, reward is likely to be completely out of the control of the experimenter. Reminiscence as a phenomenon is so meaningless and abstract that it is hard to think about.

I turn to the laboratory experiments on college sophomores or sixth grade students in a soundproof room, responding to a buzzer or a bell or a nonsense syllable. Some three hours later they were tested on Rorschach, Card VI. While sound generalizations resulted from these procedures, they were applicable only to the extent to which you could re-introduce the laboratory controls, which you never can. Therein lies the disastrous position of one who attempts to apply learning theory in actual situations.

The truth is that we have nearly always done better by changing the modes of responding rather than by accelerating or accentuating learning according to theory. Consider a situation with too many ground loops in landings with conventional type landing gear. You spend a great deal of time distributing your trials, patting the aviator on the back when he has made the landing appropriately, and watching carefully for interference and transfer. You cut down on cross wind landing accidents by two per cent. Then someone introduces a tricycle landing gear and such accidents are completely eliminated. I can only be discouraging because, in the three years I have spent at Pensacola occasionally attempting to apply learning theory, I have found no specific application of previous experiments other than indications of what variables to look for. I have never been able to apply specifically and directly any single experiment or any single finding presently existing in the realm of experimental psychology. I went through a year's *Journal of Experimental Psychology* seeking one study that could be directly applied to Naval Aviation Training. I found none. While this is likely to be a result at least in part of my own limitations, it is a rather common experience, I believe.

Our problem seems to lie in the fact that we use completely different definitions when we go from the laboratory to the workaday situation. Laboratory stimuli are often divided along dimensions of physical similarity. We cannot even tell what our stimuli are in an hour's classroom teaching.

The most discouraging experiment I have seen to date on the application of learning theory was one reported at an APA convention. Subjects were given a very simple task of learning the names of electrical symbols. Five people were called together who were described as learning theorists. They were asked to map out the most effective program possible in learning. The task amounted to learning a series of nonsense syllables, the kind of learning about which we know the most. The program introduced distributed practice, knowledge of results, reminiscence, generalization, transfer, and the like. The program was given to a group of airmen and the length of time they required to learn these electrical symbols was carefully recorded. Then the electrical symbols were given in a free learning situation to another group of airmen, and there was a slight favoring of the free learning situation over the prescribed training program. I would not have believed that finding if I myself had not done an experiment that was exactly analogous. I had subjects learning names and faces. I introduced optimal conditions as described in learning texts. I also had a free learning group. Through use of mnemonic devices, and who knows what besides, the free learning group actually learned more rapidly than the structured learning group.

Now I have gently stated a sad story. It demands action on our part because certainly there is truth coming from the laboratory. But the translation of this information to the learning situation, to my knowledge, has been among one of the most ineffective activities of the psychologist today.

Learning, Prediction, and the Simplex

Lloyd G. Humphreys

University of Illinois

[In this paper on the simplex given at a conference at Washington University in 1959, Lloyd Humphreys pointed to an impressive body of information concerning the nature of learning. Humphreys approached learning primarily from the vantage point of prediction but nevertheless took the opportunity at appropriate intervals to indicate the implications of the simplex phenomenon for education and training. Whereas most previous work pertaining to the simplex had been cross-sectional in nature, Humphreys' interest is in maturation and learning data collected over a substantial period of time. Dr. Humphreys, in permitting republication of his paper, has stated that it no longer completely represents his present thinking.]

The starting point for my paper is a paradox. On the one hand, I have observed the results of many training experiments and have been impressed by two typical findings: only small differences due to experimental treatments, and consistently large differences associated with initial individual differences. One might well conclude that learning is not a very important process, or better that the typical psychological manipulations of learning variables do not make important contributions to variance. On the other hand, ability measures are not as stable over long periods of time as one would hope for many prediction purposes, nor perhaps as stable as one might expect them to be considering their stability under experimental manipulations. Anderson (1939), for example, found that the degree of stability of intelligence test scores was consistent with the hypothesis that gains from year to year were independent of status at the beginning of each year. It is also true, I believe, that successes in making short-term predictions of socially useful criteria are somewhat counterbalanced by failures in making long-term predictions of similar criteria. Without special experimental manipulation changes take place within our subjects which substantially attenuate our long-run predictions.

Although I have started a research program concerned with the stability of individual difference measures and with the prediction of socially useful criteria over various periods of time, I have as yet no data of my own to report. My paper is therefore theoretical; or if theoretical is too high sounding a term, I will settle for speculative. I should also acknowledge the stimulation I have received from Edwin A. Fleishman and Marshall Jones.

My speculations are centered around a particular correlational matrix that Guttman (1954) has called a simplex. Descriptively a simplex is a matrix in which the highest value in a row or column is just off the principal diagonal and in which there is a monotonic decrease in the size of correlations as one moves away from the principal diagonal toward the periphery of the matrix along either the rows or the columns. Table 1 presents an example of a simplex.

Table 1

EXAMPLE OF A SIMPLEX

	1	2	3	4	5
1		95	90	86	81
2			95	90	86
3				95	90
4					95
5					

Guttman also has an analytic definition of the simplex form. This is: $r_{ik.j}$ equals zero, where j lies between i and k. My speculations refer, however, to the descriptive definition of the simplex.

Guttman (1957) discusses simplexes largely in conjunction with cross-sectional studies of psychological tests. For example, certain verbal tests form a simplex. My interest, however, is in learning or maturation data. In general, the intercorrelations of trials, phases, or other successive measures of a function changing over time form a simplex. No matter what the degree of experimental control or the homogeneity of the process, the intercorrelations will generally not fall into the hierarchical form, described by Spearman, which can be explained by a single general factor. With lack of control or heterogeneity of process the intercorrelations may not form a simple simplex.

Perhaps a bit of explanation for this generalization is in order. Note in the first place that the intercorrelations of learning or maturational phases involve in effect part-whole correlations. In some learning situations the change from trial to trial can be considered to represent a dropping out rather than the addition of responses, but this does not alter the part-whole relationship. It is only necessary to assume in addition that the change from trial to trial is less than perfectly correlated with the first of the given pair of trials. I assume, in other words, that increments or decrements are never perfectly correlated with their respective bases. The amount of change in successive correlations along a row or column will be a function of the degree of correlation between the increment or decrement and the base, and of the variance of the increment or decrement relative to the variance of the base.

Some concrete examples may be in order. With respect to learning data I expect to obtain simplexes from the intercorrelations of trials in motor skill learning, in maze running of rats, in the learning of reading or arithmetic, or in learning to fly an airplane. With respect to maturational data I expect to obtain simplexes from the intercorrelations of variables such as height, weight, and running speed, when successive measures are obtained over a period of time. Finally, since simplexes are expected for both learning and maturational data one should certainly obtain simplexes for the intercorrelations of measures of psychological traits obtained over a period of time.

The significance for prediction of the ubiquitous simplex should now be described in more detail. In longitudinal studies intercorrelations of height, of reading, of verbal ability cannot be explained by a single factor. For example, verbal tests may be relatively pure measures of verbal factors at 6 and 16, but in the longitudinal sense the same factor is not represented by the two sets of verbal tests. A minimum of two factors will always be involved. There is always a gradual reordering of individual differences between the initial and terminal points.

Although a side issue with respect to the main purpose of this paper, this phenomenon of change of function over time is exceedingly important to the experimental psychologist who arbitrarily sets criteria for learning, forgetting, and extinction. The decision of whether to analyze only the last trial in a series, or a group of several trials, should depend on the intercorrelations of those trials.

Does asymptotic performance as measured by the group means coincide with stabilization of the correlations between trials? The amount of reordering of individual differences depends of course upon the level of correlation between trials. An important class of empirical problems is the determination of when, in a given simplex, relative stability is achieved. At age 18, for example, height should be relatively stable. While the intercorrelations of height beyond age 18 might still form a simplex—some people may shrink a little, some may still grow a little—the correlation between initial and terminal status will still be relatively high. Do the intercorrelations of psychological traits ever achieve this degree of stability? If our aptitude measures are heavily loaded with learned components, they will probably be substantially less stable. Even so it is important to determine relative stability of different functions at different ages. Such information is essential for the intelligent use of psychological tests. For example, some school systems have entered children in an ungraded room from which they are promoted into the graded curriculum as they learn to read. Since the correlation between first grade reading and fourth grade reading is in the .20's (Block, 1950), such a policy is short-sighted.

Even when we are able to use predictor tests that have achieved relative stability, it is even more important to predict criteria that have achieved such stability. I need only mention in this connection the large numbers of correlations in the selection and guidance literature between aptitude tests and initial measures of training success in schools, the military, and industry, and the relative lack of such information for more remote criteria or for asymptotic performance.

The increasing use of present achievement as a predictor of future performance, e.g., high school mathematics for college freshman mathematics, needs to be evaluated more carefully than it has been heretofore. Clearly the usefulness of this procedure is a function of the stability of the simplex, since in effect we are using a measure early in learning to predict a later portion of the learning curve. A useful degree of prediction of freshman mathematics is not sufficient; senior mathematics is undoubtedly more important. In this connection it is interesting to note that an individual test of intelligence in the first grade may not be as good a predictor of second grade reading as a first grade reading test, but the former is a better predictor of fourth grade reading than the latter; that is, a measure early in learning is not necessarily the best available predictor of performance later in learning (Block, 1950).

Problems involving the simplex may be somewhat illuminated by factor-analytic models. Guttman (1954) prefers to describe simplexes in terms of triangular matrices having the same order as the correlational matrix. These triangular matrices may show either increasing

Table 2

TRIANGULAR FACTOR MATRIX DESCRIPTIVE
OF A SIMPLEX

		Factors				
		I	II	III	IV	V
	1	1.00	.00	.00	.00	.00
	2	.95	.31	.00	.00	.00
Variables	3	.90	.30	.31	.00	.00
	4	.86	.28	.30	.31	.00
	5	.81	.27	.28	.30	.31

or decreasing factorial complexity as a function of increasing trials, and the decision as to which is to be preferred must be made on logical grounds. A triangular matrix of this sort is presented in Table 2 for the correlational data in Table 1.

Although not mentioned by Guttman, one finds also that two factors give an appropriate fit for many simplex data and an exact fit, as described by DuBois (1960) for four or five variable matrices. Perhaps because of long standing habits of thought, I find a two-factor solution more interesting than an n-factor solution. Even with only two factors one has a choice of preferred rotational solutions. In any matrix in which the lowest correlation is greater than zero, the two factors will be oblique. The rotated oblique factor pattern for the data in Table 1 is presented in Table 3 along with the correlation between the two factors. Two correlated factors can, however, be equally well represented by three orthogonal factors of which the first is a general factor determined by the correlation between the two original oblique factors. This solution is also presented in Table 3. Finally, if one wishes, an arbitrary orthogonal rotation of the two factors can be obtained, the position of the axes depending on how one expects to use the data. A rotation of this sort is presented in the last two columns of Table 3.

Table 3

ALTERNATIVE ROTATIONS FOR THE TWO-FACTOR
SOLUTION OF A SIMPLEX

		Oblique		Hierarchical			Orthogonal	
		I	II	General	I	II	I	II
	1	98	00	91	36	00	50	84
	2	82	18	93	30	07	42	88
Variables	3	50	56	93	19	19	26	94
	4	18	82	93	17	30	09	97
	5	00	98	91	00	36	00	98

r = .86

Any one of these rotational solutions may prove useful theoretically and practically. As in any factor analysis it is not difficult to attach names to any of these factors. Further experimental manipulations can perhaps furnish a basis for choosing among them. I believe that one can conclude now, however, that the third rotational solution does have practical importance. The first factor is best defined by early trials. In learning data it can represent the temporary learning sets brought to the situation by the subjects. These furnish an initial advantage independent of level of performance, but this advantage is washed out as learning progresses. The second factor represents more remote performance, and if learning is carried far enough it represents asymptotic performance. In most practical prediction situations one hopes to have predictor tests loaded primarily on the second factor. I suspect that many predictors are loaded primarily on the first.

The interpretation of the three-factor hierarchical solution is also reasonable. The first group factor is interpreted as above. The second group factor is different, since it now represents terminal performance with initial performance held constant. In other words, it is now primarily a rate of learning factor whereas the second factor combined rate and level. The general factor could represent capacity independent of differences in initial learning sets and of differences in rate of learning associated with the particular learning task.

There is one obvious difficulty with these factorial interpretations, particularly with the oblique rotations or with the hierarchical solution: namely that, unless the simplex has stabilized, the positions of the axes depend on the stage of learning reached. Correlated factors, or a general factor, at one stage may give way to uncorrelated factors or a near-zero variance general factor if learning is carried far enough. This objection is not as serious for the arbitrary two-factor orthogonal solution since even if the position of the second axis is not stable it is at least close to the final one, and one would still prefer to find predictor tests that were loaded primarily on it.

The problem of predicting performance late in a simplex from data available at the beginning of the sequence is not an easy one. A look at the problem of predicting adult height from an early period in development may give us some leads as to how to proceed in other kinds of prediction problems. The first step is to recognize that height at the earlier period will be less than a perfect predictor of adult height. Although early measures from the simplex may be quite inaccurate, there are other possibilities. Parental height might be used. Other measures of physique might add to the accuracy of prediction of adult height. Physiological indices constitute still other possibilities. Estimation of future diet patterns might also add to the prediction;

that is, we might have to take into account possible environmental determinants that intervene between the time the prediction is made and the time criterion information is obtained.

Now let us turn to the problem of predicting future academic performance for children at the end of the eighth grade. Children frequently enter one of several tracks at this point, the choice among tracks being based upon aptitude and achievement information. The criterion we wish to predict is college-level achievement, but the tests are typically validated against ninth grade performance. Would measures of interest and motivation add to the prediction of the more remote criterion? Will general intelligence measures show less decrement in validity over time than the more specific predictors that are essentially achievement tests? Can we increase the accuracy of prediction if we know what kind of high school the child is going to attend, what kind of family atmosphere he will have, what sort of peer group he will belong to? I am certain that we shall have to consider questions of this type in order to move ahead in the prediction business; and psychometricians will perforce become interested in problems of maturation, learning, and motivation.

PART II

Measurement of Learning

In the measurement of learning and other psychological phenomena, we make at least three tacit assumptions. The first is that behavior can be represented numerically; the second is that the resultant numbers can be manipulated according to mathematical principles; and the third is that the results of these manipulations can provide insightful and valid representations of the behavior in question. These assumptions are implied each time we quantify a set of observations, compute descriptive statistics pertaining to the observations, and generalize to a population of subjects that have not themselves been observed. These assumptions are so much a part of the natural environment of the educational researcher that seldom does he even bother to examine them. One may argue with considerable logic, however, that it is a healthy thing to examine one's assumptions from time to time regardless of how obvious or well founded they may have been at the time they originally were accepted.

In educational evaluation we are interested in improving our methods of observation, increasing their adequacy, and in scaling them in such fashion that a numbers system can be applied meaningfully. In essence this is what the papers in this section of the monograph are all about. In viewing the natural sciences, which we often implicitly or explicitly use as a model, we note the great convenience of numbers as a tool in generalization. A considerable part of our own technical literature has to do with problems associated with inference and generalization. Additionally, our use of standard errors of various types, tests of statistical significance, and norms stems largely from the requirement to infer and to generalize. We have reasonably good procedures for making evaluative observations, as exemplified both in educational laboratory procedures and in numerous psychological tests. As a rule results are expressed in metric form; sometimes they can be considered scaled; and

51

not infrequently they provide accurate predictions of behavior of groups under consideration and of individuals on whom measures have been taken.

The initial issue of this monograph series was introduced by an article titled "Toward a Technology of the Evaluation of Educational Programs." A technology of evaluation may be considered to be essentially a part of educational engineering. The engineering model is probably as useful in developing a technology of evaluation as is the natural science model in the development of other scientific disciplines. Engineers speak of problems associated with the noise-to-signal ratio, the ratio of extraneous material to pertinent material reaching the sensor. In educational measurement we have the same problem; we call it validity. In cases of low validity we can hardly hear the signal because of the masking noise. Other engineering analogies can be found for most concepts having to do with educational measurements: for reliability, for norms, and for test interpretation. For example, a common means of increasing reliability in engineering is the use of redundancy; we employ the same principle to increase reliability of educational measures by increasing the number of essentially homogeneous items.

Most of our measures used in educational evaluation seem to be a bit better than ordinal, but not quite up to the standard of an interval scale. The distance between points on the scale often is not equal. This poses few problems with respect to reliability for additive operations, since addition normally increases reliability, but it causes complications when we attempt to subtract. Tests having satisfactory reliability often become unsatisfactory in this respect when their parts are scored separately to form subtests. On a typical test a difference of two points in raw score at the upper end of the scale may be very different from a difference of two points in raw score at the lower end of the scale. A technology for evaluating educational accomplishments should use as its point of departure the changes which actually take place from one point in time to another and then build measuring devices that are particularly responsive to the new activities which are being observed. These measures should, as previously inferred, be redundant, and hence reliable.

In the conventional engineering environment, new developments are validated against relatively clear-cut performance specifications. A device for communication or transportation performs at the level for which it was designed or it fails to do so. If it does not perform at the level specified, shortcomings are identified and corrected, or certain components are redesigned with a view to meeting performance specifications. In each instance the engineering changes that are made are based upon appropriate information from the underlying sciences. In

*educational evaluation the procedures of our technology will be some-
what less clear-cut for some time to come than in the case of conventional engineering. Similarly, scientific principles on which the technology is based will be less precise than those from the natural sciences.
Even so, when applied with imagination and ingenuity the present
technology of educational evaluation achieves a degree of success and
progress, although painfully slow, is being made. The papers included
in this section of the monograph identify a number of the problems involved and offer approaches to solutions of some of them.*

*We cannot and should not wait until we have perfected educational
evaluation procedures to apply them in the practical educational environment. The final step in educational evaluation is that of translating
statistical computations back into behavior. The abstraction that comes
from a desk calculator or a third generation computer becomes meaningful only when it functions in a very different world, namely, the
world of behavior from which the original observations came. The individual engaged in the technology of educational evaluation should be
aware that measurement, scaling, and analysis necessarily lead not only
to generalization and verification but also to application.*

Measurement of Learning in Extensive Training Programs

Wilse B. Webb

University of Florida

[One readily can infer from the content of Webb's paper that he is a psychologist with a strong experimental background who for some time conducted educational research in the very real world of aviation training. It is clear that he has come to grips with the unrelenting problems of measurement that are found in abundance in the typical educational situation. It is equally clear that Webb has been giving a great deal of sober thought to these problems, and has reached some conclusions from which most individuals engaged in educational evaluation can profit. He carefully identifies the characteristics of measurement that are desirable, those that are essential, and the midway ground of compromise that must be accepted if we are to function in the real world of education or training.

Toward the end of his paper Webb condenses the main points he has made and draws a basic conclusion. In oversimplified form, the conclusion is that adequacy of educational measurement is dependent upon the degree to which we are able to apply the learning laboratory model. But this brief statement of Webb's position definitely is not recommended as a substitute for a reflective reading of Webb's paper.]

I propose to discuss some of the problems inherent in the measurement of learning in organized and extensive training programs. By a training program I mean a systematic attempt to convey knowledges, attitudes, or skills to trainees. I have introduced the terms organized and extensive to attempt to eliminate awesome but unsystematic learning in the social context as well as the finely controlled and often finicky problems of nonsense syllables, golf lessons, and rats in mazes. In brief, I am attempting to focus our attention on what is more generally called educational programs.

A starting point would be to define in general terms, learning. Here a classical definition would seem to do—behavior changes due to practice (training). As for the dimensions of these behavior changes, I would in this context include three—knowledges, attitudes, or skills. If we understand these dimensions in a broad sense—knowledges to include understanding and insight as well as factual material, attitudes to encompass not only feelings but also sets and prejudices, and skills to range from mental problem solving procedures through motor responses —I believe we can use them effectively. Admissibly the inclusion of knowledges and attitudes as behavior stretches the classical term behavior a bit, but since their expression is only seen in behavior I consider this reasonable.

Accepting these rather innocuous generalizations, let us turn to more specific questions of what, where, and how to measure. Since the when and how are pretty certainly to be conditioned by the what one is trying to measure, let us turn to that knotty issue first.

WHAT TO MEASURE

Training programs must be directed toward conveying knowledges, attitudes, or skills to trainees in order that they may more efficiently perform some tasks or a constellation of tasks (jobs) more efficiently than would have been the case if the program had not been given. Accepting this notion, what to measure becomes, at least in theory, simple enough—we measure how well the person has learned to perform the task in question.

Of course, we encounter formidable problems. The training program may be directed toward a job both complex in character and prolonged in time. For example, a training program in accounting may involve a lifetime of complex tax decisions while a legal training program may involve a lifetime of complicated cases in the courts. Further, efficiency may take many forms. For example, a program in medicine may result in a good surgeon or dermatologist, while a pilot training program may result in a good seaplane pilot or a good helicopter pilot. In addition, this efficiency may be judged by many means which are not necessarily linearly nor highly related. For the physician this efficiency could be variously judged by income, happiness, patient satisfaction, or the number of cases treated successfully. The pilot's efficiency may be judged in terms of his ability to fly, his ability to command or to take on new aircraft, or his bravery.

Although these problems can often be surmounted by fractionation and arbitrary decisions, they become more difficult when the tasks verge on the intangible—when cultural courses are given to "enrich" the trainees' "way of life," or social science courses purportedly result in "better citizenship" or psychology courses are supposed to give the student a "better understanding of himself" or English literature courses give the trainees "a greater appreciation of good writing" or a management course "makes the person a better executive."

The problem of what to measure boils down to the necessity of developing for each program a clear-cut, unequivocal description of the tasks that the trainee is supposed to perform more efficiently as a result of his training. I would say that until we have a fairly rigorous definition of what skills, knowledges, and attitudes we expect a person to acquire from a program, the measurement of learning resulting from that program will not be very effective. Too often we see what is being measured as being primarily determined by what can be readily measured rather than what can be considered a relevant measure. In fact, what seems to usually happen is that we end up being satisfied with measuring what knowledge has been acquired since this is usually easy to do. Admissibly, knowledges are frequently propaedeutic to skills and attitudes, but let us not confuse them.

HOW TO MEASURE

The question of how to measure learning in training programs is a problem of technique involving two issues: 1) the units of measurement, and 2) the methods of measurement.

1. The Units of Measurement.   There are a number of units in which behavior can be measured. The most common are speed, accuracy, probability of occurrence, originality, persistence, amount, and correctness. The unit to be used is, of course, dependent on the critical requirements of the task or job for which the subject is being trained. If accuracy is required, accuracy must be measured; if speed is required, then speed is to be measured.

Let me make a few comments on these units of measurement as they are related to the dimensions of knowledges, attitudes, and skills.

Take knowledges, for example. Perhaps this is the easiest and hence the most frequently measured aspect of learned behavior. We typically measure knowledge in terms of accuracy (Was Shakespeare a 16th century character?), or probability of occurrence (When was Shakespeare born?), and, by inference, amount (12 questions about Shakespeare were answered out of 15). We seldom test the speed of such responses or persistence of responses although both may be extremely critical requirements for the use of the knowledge acquired.

In the case of skills we nearly always measure accuracy and speed but frequently neglect to test for their probability of occurrence in realistic environments; and persistence often goes by the board. For example, we may measure how skilled a person is in stripping a rifle for cleaning it but include no measure as to whether he will or can clean his rifle at a later date. Or we may determine whether a person can pass a German reading examination but not measure whether he will read German or can read German at some later date.

2. The Methods of Measurement. Under methods of measurement I wish to consider the broad question of objective measurement vs. subjective measurement; that is, the use of standardized stimuli and specified responses vs. judgmental assessments. It is unnecessary to catalogue here the usual advantages of objective tests or the well known disadvantages of subjective tests. Rather, I think it would be useful to point up the frequent necessity of and justifications for using subjective tests in the types of programs we are discussing.

First, we are likely to agree that an objective test which is not valid regardless of its other virtues is sometimes worse than useless.[1] It is worse in the sense of giving a false sense of security.

I have noted two situations in which objective tests run into this problem of validity and subjective tests become the necessary recourse: 1) the ultimate criterion itself (satisfactory performance of the task) has a heavy subjective loading, and 2) the task involves responding to a wide complexity of conditions with a wide variety of complex skills.

A good example of the first type of situation is one in which the trainee must learn to become a member of a group, as in an officer-training program or a part of a team, as in a crew-training program. In both instances it is critical that the person learn to adapt himself to interaction with others. How well this is done, of course, is most directly measured by the judgment of others of the individual action in relation to *them.* Here it is likely that some form of peer rating—a purely subjective measure—will be useful.

Learning to be an aviator or a better executive are examples of the second type of situation that seems to require a subjective type mea-

---

[1] By valid here is meant the simplest meaning of the term—measuring what it is supposed to measure.

sure—that is, they are situations that are quite complex. Although in both these instances specific skills may be necessary, the situations in which the skills are applied and the combinations and sequences in which the skills are employed are likely to be quite varied. In the case of the pilot, it is necessary that he learn to make a smooth coordinated turn. However, it is even more important that he know when to begin such a turn, where each turn will end up, and how such turns are related to the varying requirements of flying. These capabilities cannot be judged from the isolated ability to perform a coordinated turn under standard conditions. Instructors feel that they can tell from observing a student engaged in the general process of learning to fly a given task (for example, landing) how good a flyer the man is likely to be in the vastly varied types of situations which will be posed by landings. He would prefer this general holistic evaluation to using part task after part task involved in landing and observing the man's precise deviations from these part tasks.

WHEN TO MEASURE

And then there is the question of when to measure learning. Within the framework of this paper—that programs exist for people to learn to perform particular tasks or jobs—the most appropriate time of measurement is during the performance of the job. However, this most appropriate time usually is surrounded by problems. In the first place, the individual is frequently being trained to operate independently in geographically widespread areas on tasks in which the man matures over long periods of time. Naval aviators, for example, operate throughout the world and take some 15 years to become squadron commanders. Physicians are similarly scattered geographically and vary widely in reaching maturity of responsibility. Even restricted industrial training programs show considerable proliferation in area and timing of success. In such circumstances where the researcher has limited control over both the physical facilities for testing and the intervening opportunities for performance the problems of finding the most appropriate time of testing may be insurmountable.

Compelled to retreat, we usually measure surrogates of on-the-job performance—performance during training. We may reason quite soundly that we are training men to perform on the job and, therefore, how well they will perform the job can be inferred from training performance. We may righteously contend that those who cannot or do not learn how to perform the job, by definition, cannot do the job.

As sound as such logic is it is, like any logical proposition, dependent upon the premises involved. Here, of course, the critical premise is that performance on the skills being learned in training is in fact directly related to job performance. When reduced to specific instances the brightness of the general logic frequently tarnishes. We fail a student who cannot pass a basic math course in naval air training. How sure can we be that he could not become a pilot? Or we drop from our graduate program a student who fails statistics. Are we sure he could not become a psychologist?

My general impression is that we too often assume too much. For a sound use of the surrogates a careful assessment of the premise on which we are operating should be made. Where possible, we should make a direct test. Although it may not be possible to follow up and test all graduates of our program it may be possible to follow up some of them and extract some form of performance measure. In such a case we can test our within-training measures as surrogates of on-the-job performance and as a consequence use them more or less confidently as measures of learning to do the job on all subjects in the future. Where this is not possible, we can rigorously examine the validity of our within-training measures as facsimiles of on-the-job performance and weight their use accordingly. Or finally, we may attempt to introduce simulated on-the-job test situations within training; that is, we may increase the use of situational type tests which closely approximate the situations of job performance.

OTHER MEASUREMENT PROBLEMS

What other limits are imposed on us in our measurement of learning in complex programs? We have seen that we frequently do not know what we wish to measure. When we decide on what we wish to measure it is usually quite complex, involving literally thousands of response sequences. The situations in which the learning is to be applied are likely to be quite varied. Frequently, the true criterion of learning is not available to us until long after the training cycle. What else besets us?

The added difficulties I wish to mention can be subsumed under one term—lack of control. First, there is the matter of stimulus presentation. In the classical learning problem we can describe the stimulus complex that is being presented and in turn define a trial—the presentation of such a stimulus complex. In an extensive program this is seldom possible. Take a training flight or a classroom period as an example. The nearest thing to a definition of the stimulus is likely to be a one page description of the material to be covered during an hour. From this the instructor constructs a specific series of stimuli. In the classroom, for example, an instructor lecturing will say about 400 sentences. Each of these will be different. And for each instructor they are likely to be different. Now add the ramification of a) considerably different amounts of studying prior to the presentation, and b) differing amounts of study and recitation by the subjects following the presentation. Certainly, the concept of a trial as we have come to know it begins to lose meaning.

Then, of course, we must also acknowledge the widely varied motives present in the subjects. We know that behavior operates roughly on a habit x drive basis. We suspect that the acquisition of H is affected by D if only to the extent that reinforcement—both kind and amount—is related to D. It would follow then that wide variation in motives (D) in a training program will affect learning. As it varies erratically in large training programs our measurement of learning is likely to be erratic. Independent of the amount learned, variations in D will directly affect performance and this measure then may reflect varying amounts of learning or motivation.

These variations in motives are also likely to affect the amount of practice that a subject voluntarily imposes upon himself. Since most of the practice in prolonged programs is primarily self-controlled, it varies widely. When this is combined with the physical variations in practice conditions—good and bad instructors and scheduling variations—we can see that control of trials is quite vague.

WITHIN-PROGRAM MEASUREMENT OF LEARNING

In spite of all these difficulties we proceed and profit from the measurement of learning in training programs. We keep our units of concern small enough and we use the most available and relevant measures of acquisition. We try, and, I think, often successfully, to measure learning in segments of our programs to two ends: 1) to assess variables which affect learning, and 2) as techniques of human quality control.

1. Assessment of Learning Conditions. In both instances our procedure is to take a segment of the program for which a given performance can be somewhat adequately defined, such as acquiring information presented in 26 periods devoted to basic physics or learning to land an aircraft on a carrier. If our concern is to evaluate between one or more conditions of training we will extract a measure of performance by which we may infer the degree of response to the experience presented, that is, ability to solve certain problems based on physical principles or number of passes required to land on the carrier. We are likely to give a pretest to be able to use a covariance analysis or randomize our students and assign them to the conditions under question. For example, we may wish to determine the effectiveness of a movie presentation of the physics data vs. an instructor presentation or determine the effect of additional trials (flights) of field carrier landing practice. We then proceed to assess our differences on our measures.

Usually, the conditions which we introduce are not neatly defined and the controls over both the independent variable and the dependent variables are rather crude. Strangely enough this very crudity of the controls often adds a valuable touch of realism to the experiment. If an effect is not noted under the conditions of the experiment, it is not likely to be found in the uncontrolled world in which it must be applied.

2. *Quality Control Measures.*   The use of learning measures for quality control purposes is sometimes called secondary selection. It is a tremendous asset to most extensive (and therefore expensive) programs—sometimes formally, sometimes quite informally.

We all know that when selection tests are used to select people for complex programs lasting over periods of time, unless the selection ratio is quite low the accuracy is going to be far from perfect. When we combine imperfect initial selection with an expensive program or the requirements that the graduate of the program must operate with a high degree of effectiveness we must typically eliminate individuals within the training cycle.

The major bases for this secondary screening are measures of learning. As trainees fail the various phases of a program they are eliminated, until a graduate is one who has been able to learn all that is considered necessary in order to perform the task for which he is being trained. Recognizably, some of these failures are not failures in learning but failures of motivation or failures of the program itself; but the performance score presumably reflecting learning is the keystone of the elimination process. In other words, the man may have failed to learn for many reasons, but the fact is that he failed to learn.

To be effective, these secondary screening programs require attention. Trainees must be failed only on phases of training critical to subsequent phases of training or to the ultimate task. Adequate cutoff points must be developed for critical phases. Care must be taken to distinguish between failures due to capacity and failures due to the program. In many programs, because of the expense of extensive training, the earliest possible predictions of subsequent deficiency must be sought for exploitation. Fortunately, few of these requirements involve much theory but only straight-forward statistical procedures and dogged effort.

A SUMMING UP AND APPLICATION

I fear that my presentation has been more than a bit rambly and has been couched in such general terms as to be frustrating. Further, it has been stuffed with if's, however's, and also's. Let me try to summarize what would seem to be the ideals in measuring learning in any program and follow this by attempts at specific application.

To measure learning effectively:

1) Determine what is to be learned from the training sequence. Specify in terms of observable trainee activities.

2) Determine the units of behavior most clearly relevant to the performance of the activity.

3) Measure these behaviors as reliably as possible.

4) Measure the behaviors within the context toward which the training is directed.

5) Control the variables extraneous to the learning process.

6) Control the conditions of learning in a specifiable fashion.

I am quite sure that these dicta are familiar to my brethren of the laboratory and for that matter to the most recent graduate from a course in experimental psychology. In fact, there is probably some concern about my concern (poor old Bernie, he's looking for dead horses to beat). Regarding measurement of learning in its classical context for the psychologist—the laboratory—I can only thoroughly agree that I am flailing a dead horse. For example, I checked this impression against an experiment essentially chosen at random from the *Journal of Experimental Psychology,* "Effect of Amount of Interpolated Learning and Time Interval before Test on Retention in Rats" (Frankmann, 1957). The problem in this experiment was to find what effect varied amounts of interpolated learning and varied interpolated time periods had on original learning. To study this, behavior in the I-maze in food seeking by hungry rats was the chosen situation. In regard to the criterion outlined above:

1) Trainees were to learn to obtain food in one side of an I-maze. In the interpolated period they obtained food on the opposite side. Retention was to be measured in relation to the originally learned response.

2) Two units of behavior were selected for the measurement of retention: a) number of responses to the originally learned side, and b) reciprocal of the latency of response in the originally correct side (a correction procedure permitted this measure).

3) Photoelectric cells were used to activate timers for the response measures.

4) Tests were given to half the group five minutes after interpolated learning and to half the group 24 hours after interpolated learning.

5) All female rats were used, a 23-hour food deprivation was used which had been developed over three weeks of prehandling. Motivation at the time of testing was stringently controlled. Half the animals were run to the right and half to the left.

6) All groups were given an equal number of trials for the original learning. An intertrial interval of 30 seconds was maintained. Intervals of five minutes and 24 hours were used between test trials for two groups who had had four or 12 interpolated trials.

I would believe that in the experiment cited learning, and its cousin retention, were well and neatly measured. I would also hope that this application gives some strength to a notion that the guidelines I have chosen will result in a neat measurement of learning.

To test this last idea, however, in relation to my accepted topic, learning in extensive programs, let us select an example from such a program, field carrier landing practice.

In terms of extensive programs I have chosen a patsy—FCLP (field carrier landing practice)—which is about three weeks long, involving about 12 flights. What is to be learned is clear as a crystal, that is, to land on a carrier. In response to the typically tough problem of what is to be learned and hence measured, we can measure the performance of the pilot as he lands on the field as if he were landing on the carrier. The particular unit will be accuracy in the behavior required. So far, so good.

Learning undoubtedly takes place—some 98 per cent of the people who take FCLP training land on the carrier at the completion of training; it is doubtful if this large a number could do this without FCLP. There is considerable doubt, however, that the individual performance measures taken reflect very accurately the amount of learning acquired by each subject. One evidence which could be cited is that the FCLP grades correlated approximately .2 with performance as measured on the actual carrier landing. The reasons?

1) Much of what is being learned and more importantly of what is *not* being learned is probably not being measured.

2) Although the unit of accuracy is certainly important a number of other units are likely to be important—probability, appropriateness of attitudes, etc.

3) Subjective measures are used and one grade is given for an hour flight. Many unobservable or vaguely defined items are scored, for example, carrier sense.

4) Landing on the field is not the same as landing on a moving carrier.

5) Varying conditions of flying, such as aircraft and instructors, exist in profusion.

6) Number of flights, previous performance, and motivation are widely different.

Could learning be measured in this or similar complex programs? The extent to which we can deal with the limitations I have cited answers the questions. Will learning be measurable? After listening to myself, I am almost convinced that it not only can but will be measured. For a more certain answer, tune in to this station at a later date. We shall keep trying.

Discussion of Webb's Paper

G. Douglas Mayo

I find myself in cordial agreement with Webb, perhaps spuriously so, in that many of the observations made by both of us in recent years have been in the relatively small world of Aviation Training. But knowing how disappointed he would be if his well-conceived and picturesquely worded paper should provoke no argument, I shall express a slightly divergent opinion on a few points, as well as agreement with most.

I feel that his organization under the headings of What, How, and When to measure learning is a productive one, in that it seems to bring him to grips with most of the knottier problems of learning, and in a logical sequence. His emphasis on a clear conception, and fairly rigorous definition of what the trainee is expected to acquire is, I think, well taken. It *should* be obvious, but our everyday practices suggest that we need to be reminded.

On the subject of when to measure, the desirability of direct on-the-job measures properly is emphasized. *Validation* of training measures against on-the-job performance is recommended as the second line of defense, with a rigorous examination of face validity as a sort of last ditch stand. I would agree with this ordering in terms of desirability, but must also add a point or two to his list of the problems involved. When the situation calls for training to a high degree of proficiency on a specific job, as in the case of folding a parachute, direct measurement is quite feasible. For years our trainees have proved their proficiency as well as their confidence in their work by jumping a chute they have packed as a sort of final examination. But in our electronics school we face a more complex measurement problem. Because of the great variety of electronic equipment and rapid changes within each of the several types it is not at all feasible to teach specific equipments, and as a result of a combination of factors (including the basic complexity of the subject, time considerations, and money) it is not feasible to train to a high level of performance (such as advanced troubleshooting) on the representative equipments that are used as training vehicles. Here we have basically a transfer problem. We teach electronics fundamentals and hope that our graduate will be able to perform satisfactorily after a period of experience on the job with whatever electronics equipment his particular squadron may be using at the time. Now the on-the-job training programs vary from squadron to squadron, and within the squadrons from time to time in response to changing operating conditions, personnel transfers, and other matters. This variability in interpolated learning adds little to the peace of mind of the psychologist who is trying to use the highly desirable but equally elusive criterion of on-the-job performance.

At the outset I promised Webb that I would disagree with him on certain points, or at least pick at his paper a bit, and all I have succeeded in doing so far is to agree with him. Here is the best I can do as a critic.

The paper begins with a definition of learning which sounds concrete—*behavior changes due to practice,* or training. It implies the measurement of observable behavior. But these *behavior changes* are quickly shredded out into such abstractions as understanding, feelings, and attitudes. I do not object to the use of these concepts, which I consider highly legitimate members of the psychological family. My objection is that they do not derive readily from the concrete nature of the definition. They, like learning itself, I believe, are more appropriately considered as constructs, the existence of which is *implied* from observations, rather than defined as behavior changes as such. One may argue that changes in these important areas are as real as any others, but the difficulty of direct measurement of these abstractions raises a question concerning the advisability of uncritically including them in the treatment of more concrete, directly observable manifestations of behavior change.

Another point—doubtless most of you have seen television programs in which the private detective or US counterspy has gotten himself in so deep that it appears that the forces of evil surely will prevail on this particular occasion. Then just before the final commercial, the local police dash in to save the day. The careful cataloging of the monstrous problems that beset the measurement of learning in complex programs, followed by a happy ending to the effect that learning not only can but will be measured, somehow reminds one of these television productions. Even so, I too think that eventually the obstacles will be overcome, or outflanked. If, as Webb suggests, he is flailing a dead horse in reiterating the conditions necessary to the effective measurement of learning, then I believe this particular expired gelding is one that profitably may be flailed periodically for some time to come.

The Criterion Problem

Winton H. Manning

Educational Testing Service

[Manning points out that, despite the extensive treatment of the criterion problem in the literature, it continues to hold a central position among educational measurement problems. While we are not at all likely to solve it in any given paper, we must continue to consider various facets of the problem from different points of view and make any small gains toward its solution that may be possible. In this context Manning undertakes, with some success, to view the criterion problems in a perspective that permits somewhat increased generalizability and validity of assessment of learning outcomes.

In essence Manning proposes an extension of the multitrait-multimethod procedures described by Campbell and Fiske. He recognizes that the size and complexity of his proposal pose serious practical problems. It can hardly be disputed, however, that relatively small efforts, characterized by simplicity, have not to date made a noticeable dent in the criterion problem.]

Psychologists have been discussing the criterion problem for so many years that it seems difficult to say anything really new on the subject. To be sure, much past discussion is closely tied to research on test validation, where the obtaining of satisfactory measures of performance has been properly identified as the most difficult and fundamental problem in any selection research program. Robert Thorndike could not have put it much more strongly than when he said, "This problem is absolutely central, for other research can only be as good as that

This paper was prepared when the author was on the faculty of Texas Christian University.

criterion" (Thorndike, 1949). It seems inevitable, then, that we should from time to time return to discuss this question, even though, like the pilgrims who went to Canterbury, the principal benefits may perhaps be obtained from what transpires along the way, rather than in what may be found when we reach our destination.

There are typically two rhetorical stances one may take to approach the problem of writing a paper on the criterion problem. The first is that of a missionary who devotes his efforts to showing that our selection and construction of proficiency criteria, especially in measuring classroom learning, is ill-conceived, trivial, biased, and downright sinful. After a long and detailed exposition of our shortcomings pointing especially to the discrepancies between curricula, goals, and evaluations of achievement he exhorts to attain salvation by finding truly meaningful, relevant criteria. A second platform, often a reaction to the first, adopts the hard-headed position that we are overly introspective, perhaps even morbid, in our analysis of the criterion problem. Rather, we should take a sophisticated approach in which we admit that the problem of finding truly meaningful, relevant criteria in the larger sense is not finally solvable. What we identify as the basis for our judgment is necessarily arbitrary, and is subject to criticism only on technical grounds, frequently on the basis that it constitutes a satisfactory operational definition of the concept in question.

The truth, I think, lies somewhere in between these two radical positions—neither the missionary nor the pragmatic sophisticate are correct in their appraisal of psychological research as regards the criterion problem. Nevertheless, it is incumbent upon me to make some suggestions of ways in which the criterion problem may be placed in a perspective that will permit greater generalizability and validity of our assessments of learning.

It will become evident as I develop the one or two modest points I wish to make that my thinking on the criterion problem has been considerably influenced by Campbell and Fiske (Campbell, 1954; Campbell and Fiske, 1959), who have emphasized the necessity of convergent and discriminant validation of tests by the means of a multitrait-multimethod matrix.

Historically, experimental psychology (especially in the field of learning), has emphasized the point that operational definitions occupy a central role in theory building. The essentially literary conceptions with which the psychologist may think must be translated into an operational definition stated in terms of a test, a measuring instrument, or an objective behavioral record of some type. The behavioral record itself is further transformed into data as soon as we map it onto some kind of measuring scale. Thus, as Coombs (1963) has pointed out, the experimenter actively engages in a process in which he first selects only some of the behavior as being relevant to his concept and, secondly, transforms this record into a qualitative or quantitative expression which is still further abstracted from the original behavior. Such a process of selection and transformation is risky in that it may lose the important and retain the trivial. On the other hand, as we have seen again and again, these processes of abstraction and transformation may be the only means by which we can see clearly what is important and relevant in the situation. Essentially, this is the model which has made physics a success, and we have no doubt emulated it for that reason. The movement from concept to operation, then, is a move which all hard-headed behavioristically oriented psychologists applaud, and it is the direction of movement which is most discussed in the literature of psychology.

What about, however, the movement from operation to construct? Probably this is one of the sources of the great concern manifested about criteria in learning, especially in classroom research. What, for example, is the GPA measuring? How can we make the move from operation to construct validly? First, of course, we must dispense with an overly restrictive definition of operationism. Years ago, Bridgman (1927) pointed out that "if we have more than one set of operations, we have more than one concept, and strictly, there should be a separate name to correspond to each set of operations." In my judgment, such a view must be rejected as too narrow and constraining. Rather, we must find a ground upon which we may discover converging clusters of measures, rather than seeking complete congruence. Such a convergent operationism emphasizes as equally important the operation to construct transformation and its converse (Campbell and Fiske, 1959).

In this light, let us consider briefly a study conducted by Roff, Payne, and Moore (1954) which dealt with the analysis of a large number of parameters of motor learning. Of the 52 variables which were measured, 39 were derived from the learning curves of 175 airmen in three psychomotor tasks: the Complex Coordinator, the Rotary Pursuit, and the Multidimensional Pursuit. The 13 learning variables were essentially the same for all three tasks:

    a. sum of all trials or total score
    b. sum of first three trials
    c. sum of middle three trials
    d. sum of last three trials
    e. average slope

f. ratio of early to late slope
g. slope at $y = 1$ (initial learning rate)
h. slope at $y = 15$ (intermediate learning rate)
i. slope at $y = 40$ (terminal learning rate)
j. difference between first three trials and last three trials
k. square of difference between successive trials (performance variability)
l. variance of raw scores for the 40 trials around the mean
m. fluctuation function of raw scores around individual cumulative mean curve.

In addition, a battery of 13 paper and pencil aptitude and ability tests was also administered. The entire set of variables was then subjected to an oblique multiple group factor analysis with the result that 16 factors were defined. These were a performance factor for each of the psychomotor tasks, an early slope factor for each of the tasks, a variability factor for each of the tasks, a late slope factor for each of the tasks, and four ability factors: verbal, numerical, mechanical, perceptual-spatial. The important thing to note is that each of the factors is *method and task specific,* and further that each is independent of the ability measures. This is not unlike the results of Anderson, as reported by Campbell and Fiske (1959), in which measures of hunger, thirst, and sex drives were more highly correlated within the obstruction box or activity wheel method than were the same drives across methods or apparatus. Similar results have been widely reported and widely repressed, for the high proportion of methods variance makes quite obvious one of the sources of difficulty in moving from operation to construct in dealing with learning criteria.

Herein, it seems, must lie both the source of the criterion problem as well as the framework for handling it. There is no way that I know of by which we may extract from the variability of a variable the proportion of variance associated with the method and with the task, unless we have convergent information about the performances of subjects in a variety of tasks using a variety of methods. Such a multitask, multimethod, multivariate approach to the problem of criterion development will require a much larger investment of effort than is normally undertaken; but less than this, it seems, may be fruitless.

A serious consideration of this proposal leads to an attempt to formulate a kind of framework by which we may seek to understand the nature of the criterion measures we employ, and their generalizability across samples and across situations or contexts. Furthermore, it would have the effect, possibly, of pointing up the extent to which research designs have become routinized and stereotyped, to the detriment of our understanding and scientific productiveness. Let me invite your attention to Figure 8. Three axes are represented, each indicating an important way of viewing experimental approaches to the study of learning, especially perhaps human learning. These dimensions are: 1. a task-method-measure dimension; 2. a subject-class dimension; 3. an occasions-context dimension. It is obvious that I have combined certain ideas in a nested fashion as to make more evident

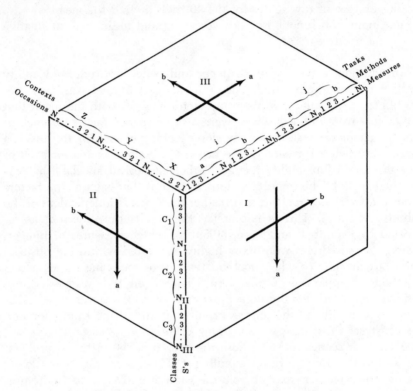

Data Class	Relationship between	Summed over	Constant Condition
Ia	Tasks-methods-measures	persons or classes	single or pooled occasions or contexts
IIIb	Tasks-methods-measures	occasions or contexts	single subjects or class of subjects
IIa	Contexts or occasions	persons or classes	single task, method, or measure
IIIa	Contexts or occasions	tasks, methods, measures	single or pooled persons or classes
Ib	Persons or classes	tasks, methods, measures	single or pooled contexts or occasions
IIb	Persons or classes	contexts or occasions	tasks, method, or measure

Figure 8. Experimental Approaches to Learning

salient aspects of the problem. Another schema for another purpose might produce a different configuration or greater utility (Gulliksen, 1958; Cattell, 1952).

One of the implications of this configuration is that we may describe at least six classes of research problems corresponding to the two surfaces which intersect in each dimension. Let me invite you to turn now to Figure 9 which deals with what seems historically the most important problem for criterion development, namely the task-method-measure dimension.

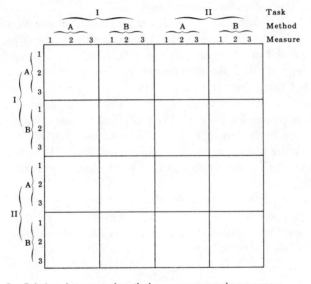

Ia   Relations between task-method-measures summed over persons for a given occasion or context.

IIIb   Relations between task-method-measures summed over occasions or contexts for an averaged (rarely single) person or class of persons.

Figure 9. The Task-Method-Measure Dimension in Learning

TASK-METHOD-MEASURE DIMENSION

A consideration of the task-method-measure matrix in Figure 9 suggests two kinds of data of interest. First, we may speak of the data generated by an obtaining relationship between task-method-measures for a particular occasion or context, and summing over a number of persons, as data Ia. On the other hand, we could obtain the inter-relationships of a task-method-measure variable for a particular person or class of persons over a number of occasions and contexts. This would be data IIIb. The second type of data is less frequently obtained, but is relevant, for example, to the question of whether the course of improvement or susceptibility to change as a function of contextual differences is parallel or similar for different tasks, methods, or measures for a particular class of learners. This is a second way of investigating the similarity structure, so to speak, of different criteria of learning, for by this means we may see how these variables behave similarly over time. Furthermore, we may compare individuals or groups of subjects, since such an approach implies that points along this latter dimension are parameters.

Although the classroom situation may present itself as an obvious example of data Ia let us consider a case in rote learning as provided in the work of Robert Stake (1958). In Tables 4 and 5 are found the intercorrelations of three parameters of the learning curves of 240 children for three rote memory tasks. Task I involves the matching of a stimulus word displayed in a window to a response word found on a switch panel. Task II is also individually administered, and involved the subject's writing down of as many of a list of 16 verbs as he could in any order, after hearing these read. Task III is the same except that the task is administered in a group and the words are adjectives rather than verbs.

In this example task and method are not separable, but the picture presented is probably illustrative of the general situation in regard to learning measures. Measures are to a considerable degree both task specific and measurement specific, in ways which are not wholly pre-

Table 4

INTERCORRELATIONS OF THREE PARAMETERS
FOR THREE TASKS

		I (Word Match)			II (Word Memory 1)			III (Word Memory 2)		
		E (error)	C (curve)	F (fit)	E (error)	C (curve)	F (fit)	E (error)	C (curve)	F (fit)
I	E	—	47	15	36	25	00	42	17	15
	C	47	—	19	23	15	−03	29	24	−06
	F	15	19	—	02	02	02	07	06	−06
II	E	36	23	02	—	89	−22	66	42	14
	C	25	15	02	89	—	−20	48	40	−06
	F	00	−03	02	−22	−20	—	14	16	15
III	E	42	29	07	66	48	14	—	74	−11
	C	17	24	06	42	40	16	74	—	−15
	F	15	−06	−06	14	−06	15	−11	−15	—

Source: Stake, 1958.

and, of course, unique variance. For example, in a classroom situation we might speak of:

a. common factors underlying general achievement in a broad spectrum of learning activities,
b. factors associated with particular tasks, say different subject matter areas, such as mathematics, English, reading, and foreign languages,
c. factors associated with methods, say objective tests, peer ratings, self ratings, teacher ratings, essay tests, and so forth,
d. and factors associated with measures, such as final proficiency, improvement in proficiency, and retention or relearning measures.

It would be a mistake to suppose that very much could be accomplished by submitting a haphazard collection of tasks, measures, and methods to such an analysis. However, by carefully defining first the domain in which we are interested, fruitful results might be obtained. Consider, for example, one of the schools of the Naval Air Technical Training Command. Could we not find portions of the existing curriculum of a school in which we could identify say four kinds of tasks: (1) a verbal rate task, (2) a nonverbal rate task, (3) a verbal relational task, (4) a nonverbal or performance relational task? Methods of assessment might include objective test scores, ratings by fellow students, ratings by superiors, and evaluations of attainment by means of programmed instructional devices. Measures could include achievement in school, rate or change measures in school, and retention measures. This would alone produce a total of 48 variables, the analysis of which by the means we have briefly implied would be likely to be productive in assessing the criteria of learning in these schools. Extension of this approach to operational fleet contexts would also be possible.

SUMMARY

In summary, we are suggesting that the criterion problem stems at least in part from our difficulty in generalizing from the available operational measures to meaningful constructs. Our principal difficulty, it seems to me, is not that we are doing the wrong things, but that we are not doing enough. An extension of the Campbell and Fiske approach to thoroughgoing analysis of our criterion data within a multitask-multimethod-multimeasure matrix offers promise as a means of developing convergent understanding of the criterion structure. Nothing inherent in the nature of the problem would prevent us from extending this framework to include a temporal dimension reflecting occasions and contexts or an individual differences dimension comprising subjects, classes, or species of subjects. In placing our emphasis on such a multidimensional matrix format, we have not meant to suggest that simply multiplying our measures will assist us. On the contrary, as measures, task, and method are increased an increased burden of logical, relational constraints should be placed upon us. Otherwise it appears unlikely that we shall do much more than throw sand in our eyes. Nevertheless, it is sobering to consider that perhaps even the simplest learning situation is too complex for such an undertaking.

Problems Arising from the Unreliability
of the Measuring Instrument

Frederic M. Lord

Educational Testing Service

[Lord begins his paper with a hilltop view of measurement in psychometrics as compared with other disciplines, and refers back to such comparisons from time to time in a constructive way as he focuses on specific problems of unreliability in the area of educational and psychological measurement. Included are instances in which corrections for attenuation are misleading, and in which observed scores and true scores do not have the same rank order to the usual, convenient, degree.

Lord emphasizes the importance of adequate estimates of true scores in educational evaluation, and especially in instances in which gain due to tuition is involved. His paper, as a whole, is one of the more lucid and incisive treatments of this topic. Fortunately, Lord does not confine his comments to telling what is wrong with educational evaluation from the standpoint of unreliability of measures but goes on to show how to make the best of a bad situation. This is accomplished primarily through the use of partial correlation between a third variable and final status with initial status held constant.]

I frequently think that the main features that distinguish statistical problems in psychometric work from the problems encountered in ordinary statistical theory arise from the presence of sizable errors of measurement in most of the variables with which the psychologist has to deal. Classical statistics has developed various devices for dealing with errors of measurement, but to date the surface of the problem has just been scratched. The psychologist is in a better position than most social scientists with respect to errors of measurement because in many situations he can produce duplicate measuring instruments each of which, to a close approximation, has the same distribution of errors of measurement. The economist, for example, typically cannot produce duplicate measures of total national income, national wealth, or consumer price level; consequently he must use the indices at hand without any direct information as to the size of the errors of measurement.

I will mention an illustration. One of the most important types of measuring instruments in the field of aptitude testing is a test of so-called quantitative ability. Examples are the Q-score on the old ACE psychological examination, the M-score on the College Board Scholastic Aptitude Test, and more recently the quantitative score on the School and College Ability Test.

It would seem very natural to ask whether these three tests actually measure the same thing or not. It is a startling fact that no one knows a theoretically adequate way to answer this question. We know that the tests do not correlate perfectly, but could it be that the lack of perfect correlation is due to errors of measurement? The standard procedure would be to try to estimate what the correlation between two of the tests would be if there were no errors of measurement—in other words, to estimate the correlation between the true scores on two of the tests. This is conventionally done by correcting their correlation for attenuation. If the corrected correlation between true scores is 1.00, then we say that the two tests are measuring the same thing.

There are two things wrong with this procedure. The first is that we do not know enough about the sampling fluctuations in the correlation corrected for attenuation. If the corrected correlation is .95, is this deviation from 1.00 merely the result of sampling fluctuations, or does it prove that the two tests do not measure the same thing? A significance test has recently been devised that will answer this question in one type of situation, but for many types of situations the question still remains unanswered.

The second difficulty with this procedure arises because all the correlations considered up to this point are product-moment correlations, which are appropriate only in the case where the regressions are linear. The correlation corrected for attenuation between two tests may fall short of 1.00 solely for the reason that this coefficient is an inappropriate measure of curvilinear relationship. If two tests have a perfect curvilinear relationship, they are still measures of the same thing, but the correlation corrected for attenuation will not disclose this fact.

I am frequently asked why two tests of the same trait should have a nonlinear relationship. I think the answer is that even though two tests are composed of similar types of items, their true scores will have a curvilinear relationship whenever the distribution of item difficulty in the two tests is different. An obvious illustration is shown in Figure 10.

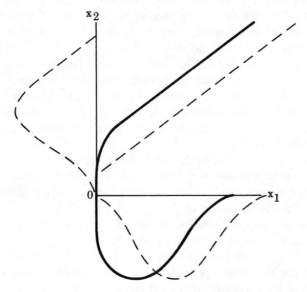

Figure 10. Regression (Solid Line) of a Test of Average Difficulty (x_2) on a Difficult Test (x_1)

Suppose first that we have two similar tests of the same ability, as represented by the dotted lines in Figure 10. The dotted straight line represents the regression of x_2 on x_1, and the dotted curved lines represent the approximately normal frequency distribution of the test scores. Suppose now that each item in the first test is made considerably more difficult, so that now there is a piling up of scores at or near zero, as indicated by the skewed frequency distribution shown as a solid curve below the x_1 axis. Since no one now obtains a very high score on x_1, the upper part of the regression line must be moved to the left, as shown in the figure. Since no one can obtain a score of less than zero, the lower part of the regression line cannot move to the left and must thus become curved, as shown by the solid regression line in the figure. Since many people now obtain scores near zero, the curved part of the regression is a significant feature of the scatterplot. It is thus clear that true scores will tend to have a nonlinear relationship whenever the two tests are at different difficulty levels.

Imagine a physicist who busily produces measuring instruments, but is unable to determine whether or not any two of his instruments are measuring the same physical dimension! This is precisely our position as long as we cannot tell whether or not two tests are measures of the same trait. For many purposes, we can and do ignore this sort of difficulty. If experience shows us that a certain test score is related to some criterion that we are anxious to predict, then we can effectively use the test score to predict the criterion. Such results are of great practical utility, but their contribution to the science of psychology is merely to point out a direction for further investigation. The observed test score inevitably contains an error of measurement, but any truly scientific interest in the score can be concerned only with that part of the score that is not error of measurement. In other words, an observed score is of scientific interest only insofar as it contains information about the corresponding true score.

Unfortunately, our methods for making inferences from observed scores to true scores are very inadequate as yet, as illustrated by the example just described. The usual method of estimating the true score of an examinee is by means of the equation $\zeta_a - \bar{z} = r_{zz} (z_a - \bar{z})$, where z_a is the actual test score of examinee a, ζ_a is the corresponding true score, $\bar{z}$ is the mean of the actual scores in the group tested, and r_{zz} is their reliability coefficient. This equation is simply an ordinary regression equation, since the test reliability can be shown to be equal to the regression of true score on observed score.

On first consideration, it seemed to me that this equation was about as good as one could wish for estimating true scores. But is it safe to assume, as this equation does, that the regression of true score on observed score is rectilinear? Consider Figure 11, which is intended to represent a rather peculiar group of examinees half of whom have true scores at ζ_0 and half at ζ_1.

The frequency distribution of observed scores for each half of the group is represented in the figure by an approximately normal curve, which must be visualized as perpendicular to the page. Since the average error of measurement is zero, the mean of each normal curve lies on the 45-degree broken line, which is therefore the regression of observed score on true score. It is graphically evident from the figure that the other regression—the regression of true score on observed score—must look like the heavy ogive-shaped line and must be very sharply curvilinear.

This figure illustrates the need for a method of estimating the examinees' true scores without assuming linear regression, as the conventional formula does. Such a method for making inferences about true scores has recently been devised as part of a project sponsored by the Office of Naval Research.

But why do we need to estimate the true scores of the examinees? We frequently get along very well in practice by ignoring true scores and working with observed scores. This happens because the rank order of the observed scores in most situations will be the same as the rank order of the best estimates of the true scores. In many practical situations, only the rank order of the true scores, not their actual value, is important. This is very convenient. It therefore comes as somewhat

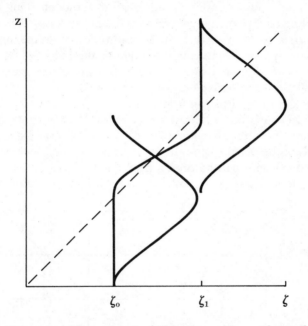

Figure 11. Regression (Heavy Line) of True Score (ζ) on Obtained Score (z) When True Score Has a Dichotomous Frequency Distribution

of a shock to learn that no such convenient situation exists when we wish to measure growth. Suppose that some test of achievement is administered to a group of students before training and that a parallel form of the same test is administered after training. Let us take the difference between posttest and pretest score for any individual and call this his *observed gain*. Now the observed gain is likely to contain large errors of measurement. We can be interested in the observed gain only because it allows us to make inferences about the *true gain*, which is defined as the difference between true score on the posttest and true score on the pretest. The unfortunate fact is that rank order of the students on observed gain is usually *not* the same as their rank order on estimated true gain.

In considering problems arising from the unreliability of the measuring instrument (which is my title), it is always helpful to compare a situation where we have errors of measurement with a parallel situation where there are no errors of measurement. For the latter situation, let us assume that the body weight in pounds of each student has been determined at the beginning of the training period and again at the end. These data might form a scatterplot such as is shown in Figure 12.

There is no problem in this situation—all the students lying above the diagonal line have shown a gain in weight and all those below the line have shown a loss in weight. It is interesting to note in passing that all those people whose initial weight was above the point w^* have experienced a loss in weight; this is the consequence of the statistical phenomenon known as regression toward the mean.

Exactly the same situation is present in Figure 13, except that here the data are supposed to be test scores rather than weights in pounds. All students above the diagonal have a positive observed gain, denoted by g, and all those below the diagonal have a negative observed gain.

What conclusions can be drawn from Figure 13 about the true gain of any student whose scores are known? More information is needed

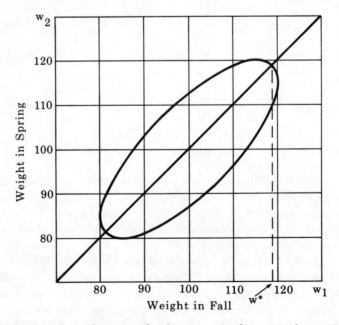

Figure 12. Hypothetical Scatterplot between Student Weight in Fall and Weight the Following Spring

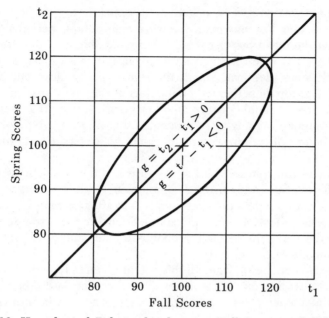

Figure 13. Hypothetical Relationship between Fall Scores and Subsequent Spring Scores

before this question can be answered. Specifically, what is needed is a scatterplot showing what the relationship between pretest and posttest would have been if no time had elapsed between the two testings. An approximation to such a scatterplot might be obtained, for example, by administering both tests one after the other to a second group of students exactly comparable to the first group. The general nature of such a scatterplot can, in fact, be inferred to a considerable extent from a knowledge of the parallel-forms reliability coefficient of the test, since this coefficient is theoretically the correlation between the two forms when they are administered almost simultaneously. If the two scatterplots are placed side by side, one showing the relationship between the two tests when several months of training intervene and the other showing the relation when they are administered simultaneously, then it follows logically that any difference between the two scatterplots must be due to something that happened during the training period. If there is no other obvious explanation of the differences between the two scatterplots, we may be willing to attribute such differences to the effect of training.

To take an extreme example, suppose that the two scatterplots are exactly alike. In this case, the only possible inference is that the training had no effect. For any given examinee, no matter whether his observed gain was positive or negative, the conclusion must be the same: that he neither lost nor gained during the training period. Suppose, next, that the mean posttest score is ten points higher when training is given than it is when no training is given, but that otherwise the two scatterplots are identical. This is the result that would occur if everyone in the group gained exactly ten points during the course of training. Since this result could occur in no other plausible way, the inference to be drawn regarding any given student is that he gained ten points during the course of training, no matter what his observed gain may have been.

Figure 14 illustrates a third situation. Here the data obtained when the two tests are administered simultaneously are indicated by the dotted ellipse; the data obtained before and after training are indicated by the solid ellipse. It is graphically evident that the training period produced a real gain among the poorer students and a real loss among the better students.

The main conclusion from all this is that given only pretest and posttest scores, without any information as to the relationship between test and simultaneous retest, no adequate inference can be drawn about the true gain for any individual.

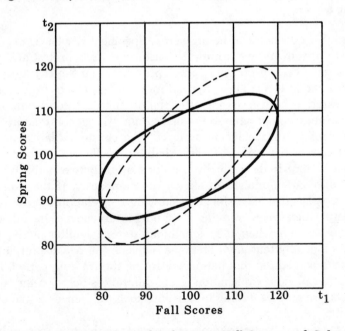

Figure 14. Hypothetical Relationship between Fall Scores and Subsequent Spring Scores (Solid Ellipse) Compared to the Relation Existing When the Two Tests Are Administered Simultaneously (Broken Ellipse)

If the pretest and posttest are assumed to be parallel forms, and if the test-retest reliability coefficient is known, then estimates of the true gain of each individual can be obtained, providing rectilinear regressions can be assumed. The method for doing this is simply to set up a multiple regression equation for predicting the unknown true gain from the two available known quantities, the pretest and posttest scores. The variance of the true gain and the correlation of the true gain with pretest and with posttest scores can all be inferred by conventional psychometric theory, so there is no difficulty in determining the values to be used for the multiple regression coefficients.

The results of applying such a multiple regression technique to actual data are shown in Figure 15. The estimated true gain of each examinee is determined by the band in which he falls.

Two things may be pointed out. First, although the true gain is the difference between two true scores, the best estimate of this difference is not the same thing as the difference between the best estimates of the two true scores. Secondly, the estimated true gain for an individual does not necessarily even have the same sign as his observed gain—an individual with a negative observed gain, for example, may nevertheless

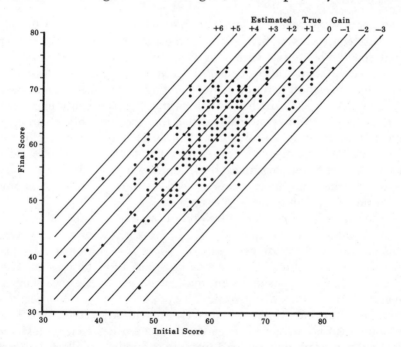

Figure 15. Scatterplot between Initial and Final Scores, with Lines Drawn to Show Estimated True Gains (Reproduced by permission from *Educational and Psychological Measurement*, 1956, 16, 434.)

have a positive estimated true gain. This last is illustrated in Figure 15 by the fact that the oblique lines are not 45-degree lines. Thus the rank order of the examinees on the observed gain is *not* in general the same as their rank order on estimated true gain. It follows that one cannot have any adequate estimate of the gains of individual examinees unless he has available and utilizes information about the reliability of the tests administered.

The question is often asked: cannot analysis of covariance methods be used to estimate the gain of individual examinees? The answer is that analysis of covariance methods, at least as ordinarily used, make no allowance for the unreliability of the predictor measure. They are inadequate for this purpose—and, incidentally, for many other purposes for which they are commonly used in educational research, for this same reason.

Up to now I have been talking about the problem of estimating the true gain for individual students. Let me go on now to another problem, the problem of estimating the correlation between gain and some other measure. This can be accomplished by very routine methods— without the novel methods used for estimating the true gain of a single examinee.

Attempts to correlate various variables with gain have led to considerable controversy, particularly in the field of personality testing. There seem to be quite a variety of ways in which the use of gain may involve either statistical or logical difficulties. Suppose it is desired to know the correlation between initial standing and gain for some specified group of students. If the variable in question is reliably measured, as is the case with physical weight, then the research worker can compute and interpret the correlation without hesitation. In the case of test scores, which are not perfectly reliable, the situation illustrates very nicely the sort of problem that arises from the unreliability of measuring instruments, and the consequent need for thinking in terms of true scores rather than in terms of observed scores.

If the research worker correlates pretest score with observed gain, he is correlating t_1 with the quantity $t_2 - t_1$. Now it is known that t_1 contains an error of measurement, say, e_1. There is also an error of measurement, e_2, in t_2, but this error may be ignored for the present. If e_1 appears in t_1 with a positive sign, then, of necessity, it appears in the quantity $t_2 - t_1$ with a negative sign; if e_1 appears in t_1 with a negative sign, then it appears in the quantity $t_2 - t_1$ with a positive sign. Thus there tends to be a spurious negative correlation between pretest and observed gain. This fact, which I am sure is familiar to all of you, was first pointed out by Sir Godfrey Thomson (1924). His article contains the necessary formulas for eliminating the spurious effect and estimating the correlation between initial standing and true gain.

In the usual situation where it is desired to correlate gain with some measure other than initial or final score, there is ordinarily no spurious effect, and the desired correlation may be computed by very familiar methods. Consider, first, the simple product-moment correlation between any predictor variable, c, and observed gain. This correlation, $r_{cg} = r_{c(t_2 - t_1)}$, can be interpreted in straightforward fashion as just what it is—the correlation between the variable c and the observed gain. Since the variable g is likely to be much less reliably measured than most ordinary test-score variables, it may be desirable to correct the correlation for attenuation. Denoting the true gain by γ, the corrected correlation is $r_{c\gamma} = r_{cg} / \sqrt{r_{gg}}$, where r_{gg} is the reliability of the observed gain. This reliability is readily computed from the pretest and posttest reliabilities and from the correlation between pretest and posttests by standard formulas given in Gulliksen's *Theory of Mental Tests* (1950).

It may be noted in passing that the estimated correlation between a third variable and true gain is not the same as the actual correlation between a third variable and estimated true gain; the way to estimate the correlation of a third variable with true gain is to use the formula for correction for attenuation, not to estimate the true gain for each examinee and then correlate these estimates with the third variable.

It is implicit in the use of the word gain that the initial and final measures are expressed in the same metric. In the case where the variable under consideration is the student's weight in pounds, there seems to be little question but that the initial and final measures are expressed on the same scale. In the case of test scores, this may not be so obvious. Even though the pretest and posttest consist of the same test questions and are physically identical, it is quite possible to maintain that the student has changed drastically during the course of instruction and that, even though we eliminate practice effect from consideration, the test no longer measures the same thing when given after instruction as it did before instruction. If this is asserted, then the pretest and posttest are measuring different dimensions and no amount of statistical manipulation will produce a measure of gain or of growth.

Suppose, for example, that at the beginning of the instruction we have measured the students' ability in arithmetic and at the end of the instruction we have measured the students' ability in algebra, and suppose that we want to know the relation between effectiveness of training in algebra and some third variable. A common but fallacious procedure that still causes much controversy and that has cast a pall of doubt over the whole use of gains, is to correlate the third variable with the difference between the *standardized* algebra score and the standardized arithmetic score.

Now, the difference between standardized score on algebra and standardized score on arithmetic is a statistical artifact with various undesirable properties. If we are trying to measure the effect of training in algebra, we are not really interested in any such statistical artifact. There may be situations where we are actually interested in such difference scores, even though the two tests do not measure the same dimension, but for most problems we must abandon the difference score and resort to partial correlation techniques. We must compute the partial correlation between the third variable, c, and the posttest, t_2, with the pretest, t_1, held constant. It will simplify matters to consider the case of normally distributed variables. In this case, this partial correlation, denoted by $r_{ct_2 \cdot t_1}$, is equal to the ordinary correlation between c and posttest for any group of people having a constant pretest score.

What is the relationship of this partial correlation coefficient to the correlation between c and observed gain? Or to the correlation between c and true gain? One difference is that the use of gain by definition supposes that pretest and posttest have the same metric, whereas no such assumption is necessary with the use of partial correlation.

The presence of errors of measurement will only serve to complicate the discussion at this point. All correlations under discussion, including the partial correlation coefficient, can be and should be corrected for attenuation. A comparison can be made most clearly, however, if we consider only perfectly reliable measures, such as physical weight measured in pounds. What, then, is the relation between $r_{cw_2 \cdot w_1}$ and $r_{c(w_2 - w_1)}$? The results of this comparison may seem paradoxical, so I hope you will watch closely to be sure that I am not hiding something up my sleeve.

The general relationship between these two correlations is too complicated to be of help here. Instead, let us ask what can be inferred about the partial correlation in the special situation where the correlation of the third variable with gain is zero.

We are going to be concerned only with the sign of the partial correlation and not with its magnitude. Thus we can simplify matters by working with the part correlation $r_{c(w_2 \cdot w_1)}$ instead of the partial correlation $r_{cw_2 \cdot w_1}$ since these two always have the same sign. As pointed out in DuBois' *Multivariate Correlational Analysis* (1957), the part correlation is by definition equal to the correlation between an ordinary variable and a residual. In this case, $r_{c(w_2 \cdot w_1)} = r_{c[(w_2 - \overline{w_2}) - b(w_1 - \overline{w_1})]}$, where $\overline{w_1}$ and $\overline{w_2}$ are the mean values for the group and b is the ordinary regression coefficient for predicting w_2 from w_1. The quantity in brackets is a residual, that is, it is the deviation of w_2 from the regression line used to predict it from w_1. Since adding or subtracting a constant to all the values of a variable will not alter its correlation with some other variable, the means in the foregoing equations may be omitted, leaving the simpler result $r_{c(w_2 \cdot w_1)} = r_{c(w_2 - bw_1)}$. Note that I have not assumed w_2 and w_1 to be expressed in terms of standard scores since such an assumption would destroy the meaning of the difference $w_2 - w_1$ as the gain in weight.

Since we are concerned only with the sign of the partial or part correlation, we can replace each correlation coefficient by the corresponding covariance. Consider $s_{cw_2 \cdot w_1} = s_{c(w_2 \cdot w_1)} = s_{c(w_2 - bw_1)}$. The partial correlation will have the same sign as this last covariance, which is readily written as $s_{c(w_2 - bw_1)} = s_{cw_2} - bs_{cw_1}$.

This last expression is readily compared with the covariance between variable c and gain: $s_{c(w_2 - w_1)} = s_{cw_2} - s_{cw_1}$. It is clear that the two covariances differ because of the coefficient b. Now

$$b = \frac{s_{w_1}}{s_{w_2}} r_{w_1 w_2},$$

by the usual formula for a regression coefficient, where s_{w_1} and s_{w_2} are standard deviations. Since the correlation $r_{w_1 w_2}$ will be less than 1, b will also be less than 1 as long as the standard deviation of the w's for the group does not increase sharply between the initial and final measurements.

The two covariances being compared differ by the quantity $(1 - b)s_{cw_1}$. *Assuming that b is less than 1,* as will usually be the case, we have the following result: *if the correlation between c and gain in weight is zero, then the partial correlation $r_{cw_2 \cdot w_1}$ will always have the same sign as the correlation between c and w_1.* For example, under the conditions stated, any third variable that has a positive correlation with initial weight will also have a positive partial correlation with final weight when initial weight is held constant.

Manning and DuBois in their report titled "Gain in Proficiency as a Criterion in Test Validation," studied the relationship of various predictors to gain in performance measured by parallel forms of an achievement test. They found that observed gain, $t_2 - t_1$, had almost zero correlation with each of their predictors and that residual gain, $t_2 - bt_1$, had significant positive correlation with each of their predictors. This latter result is what must be expected according to the foregoing algebra.

The fact that predictors correlate more highly with residual gain than they do with observed gain does not mean that residual gain is a better measure of gain than is observed gain. To return to physical weight, the difference $w_2 - w_1$ *is* the gain in weight; the residual $w_2 - bw_1$ is *not* the gain in weight, except of course in the unusual case when b is equal to 1. The fact that various predictors correlate more highly with the residual than they do with gain is a result of the correlation of the predictor with initial standing.

At this point it would be natural, but incorrect, to conclude that the partial correlation coefficient under discussion can have no important place in a study of growth. To complete the paradox, it now remains to show that although this partial correlation does not represent the correlation between the predictor and gain for the group of individuals measured, nevertheless this partial correlation coefficient is for most purposes a preferable measure of the relationship between predictor and gain.

Again assuming multivariate normality, we can state that in any group of individuals each of whom has the same weight initially, the correlation between predictor and final weight is equal to the partial correlation $r_{cw_2 \cdot w_1}$. In other words, this partial correlation is the correlation between c and w_2 for any group of individuals having a fixed w_1. It is also true that when w_1 is fixed, the gain, $w_2 - w_1$, is perfectly correlated with w_2. Thus

$$r_{cw_2 \cdot w_1} = r_{cw_2}, \text{ when } w_1 \text{ is fixed};$$
$$\text{also, } r_{cw_2 \cdot w_1} = r_{c(w_2 - w_1)}, \text{ when } w_1 \text{ is fixed}.$$

Consider now the following dilemma. We have a group of individuals in which predictor and observed gain are uncorrelated so that $r_{c(w_2 - w_1)}$ $= 0$ *for the total group*. We have already found that if the predictor is positively correlated with w_1, then we may expect the partial correlation to be positive; hence, *when* w_1 *is fixed*, $r_{c(w_2 - w_1)} > 0$. In a word, the predictor is uncorrelated with gain in the total group but the predictor is positively correlated with gain in every subgroup obtained by sectioning the total group on initial weight. The mere existence of such a situation is confusing enough.

Now suppose the predictor, c, represents the amount of vitamins added to the diet between the initial and final weighing of the students. We are anxious to increase the weight of the students and we wish to know whether adding vitamins to their diet will achieve this result. We discover that the amount of vitamins eaten is uncorrelated with gain in weight for the total group but that it is positively correlated with gain in weight for every subgroup of the total group. What do we conclude as to the value of the use of vitamins? And why?

At first sight, I found this dilemma quite incredible. Perhaps it should not appear so, since its resolution follows a familiar line of reasoning. DuBois, for example, resolved it some time ago in the course of his work.

Suppose that a controlled experiment was made with infants all of whom had the same weight at birth, and suppose it was found that the amount of vitamins eaten was correlated with gain in weight for either sex studied separately, but that there was no correlation when the two sexes were combined into a single group. In such a case, the results of interest are clearly those obtained when sex is held constant —in such a study, one avoids combining heterogeneous groups whenever possible. The conclusion suggested by the data would be that the addition of vitamins to the diet *does* tend to produce a gain in weight, even though amount of vitamins is uncorrelated with gain in weight in the total group.

Just as it is important to hold sex constant in such an experiment, so also is it important to hold initial weight constant. All the subjects could be separated into subgroups according to initial weight and each subgroup studied separately; it is usually more convenient, however, to achieve this result by the use of partial correlation techniques.

The conclusion is that when one wishes to study the effect of some outside variable on gain in weight, or on gain in test score, the ordinary correlation between the outside variable and gain is not the coefficient of primary interest. For reasons that arise from the logic of the problem rather than from any purely statistical considerations, the decisive coefficient is the partial correlation between the third variable and final status with initial status held constant. Partial correlation techniques seem to have been neglected in many cases where they are required. These techniques, it seems to me, deserve to be widely taught and frequently put into practice, especially in studies of the relation of outside variables to growth.

Measuring Gain from a Common Point of Mastery

Floyd L. Ruch

University of Southern California

[Ruch's paper addresses itself to problems associated with the measurement of learning. After identifying several major fallacies in traditional measures of gain, he describes two procedures, both of which stem from common points of mastery on the learning curves of the individual learners. Several applications of the method of bringing learners to a common point of mastery of material before measuring subsequent learning are described. Encouraging results were achieved in each instance. He expresses the view that the procedure overcomes most, if not all, of the difficulties pertaining to traditional procedures of measuring learning ability.]

This discussion of methods appropriate to research in classroom learning gives me an opportunity to reopen a problem which was of interest to me some thirty years ago, but which I had put aside because other projects have kept me busy. As a graduate student at Stanford University, I became interested in problems that required a valid definition of learning ability. Among these were the problem of the relationship between initial performance on a task and rate of gain in the mastery of that task. Another problem was the relationship between ability to learn one type of task and ability to learn another.

The traditional measure of gain from practice expresses this as the difference between performance on the final trial and performance on the initial trial. In this way learning ability is defined in terms of the amount of gain produced per unit of practice. Thus, if Subject A places 40 pegs in a pegboard in his first minute of practice and 60 in his twentieth minute of practice, he would receive the same score as another subject who placed 60 in the first minute and 80 in the twentieth minute. I feel that this measure is faulty and that the numerous studies which have employed it are largely valueless in giving us an understanding of learning ability, its causes and correlates.

One of the best established facts in the psychology of learning is that the learning curve, particularly in its final phase, is one of negative acceleration, or diminishing returns from practice. It is also reasonable to suppose that each subject entering a formal learning experiment in which his output per unit of practice is recorded enters this experiment with differing amounts of prior practice. Putting these two facts together, we see that the subject who has a considerable amount of prior practice is handicapped relative to another subject of equal learning ability who has had less prior practice. The subject with a smaller amount of prior practice enters the formal experiment during the phase of rapid acceleration, whereas the subject with a larger amount of prior practice enters the formal learning experiment nearer his physiological limit, where his curve is not accelerating as rapidly. This effect reduces correlations between initial performance and rate of gain.

If, on the other hand, we are testing the hypothesis of general learning ability, the traditional measure of learning ability is also deceptive. Suppose that Subject A has had a chance to practice Task 1 but has not had a chance to practice Task 2 before being engaged in a learning experiment involving both. His gain score on Task 1 as measured by the traditional method would be spuriously low, since he is higher on his curve and has less distance to go. This would make for low correlation between Task 1 and Task 2 and hence would point wrongly to specificity rather than generality of learning ability. Thus, for example, Woodrow's study published in 1939 reporting a factor analysis of learning scores in several tasks in which learning was defined in the traditional way gave no indication of any general learning ability (Woodrow, 1939). Nor could it be expected to. Factor analysis is a method of finding meaningful relationships among data that are meaningful in themselves. Factor analysis cannot bring meaning to basic data that are inherently meaningless.

There is another traditional definition of learning ability which does not help us either. This is the one that expresses improvement as a percentage of the initial score. Using this method, we would assign to the first subject—the one who improved from 40 to 60—a rating of 50 per cent and to the second—the one who improved from 60 to 80—a rating of 33⅓ per cent. This approach would make one subject look better than the other, whereas the first approach would make them look equally good. Neither conclusion is warranted, since neither definition of learning ability is valid. To say that improvement from a score of 40 to one of 60 represents a gain of 50 per cent is as misleading as the statement that 110° centigrade is 10 per cent hotter than 100°. However, in the case of temperatures the absolute zero point is known and can be used in the computation of the percentage of change in temperature. In the case of learning measures, the percentage method is also invalid because it assumes that the arbitrary zero point of the test coincides exactly with the absolute zero point of the ability being considered. We would only be adding further confusion to an already confused definition of learning ability, were we to use this method.

There is still another problem which must be solved before we can assign learning ability scores to subjects on the basis of their performance of a task under controlled conditions, and that is the problem of units. A raw score difference of ten points at one end of the scale is not necessarily equal to a raw score difference of ten points at the other end. The elimination of the first error in a learning experiment does not necessarily have the same significance as a measure of ability to learn as does the elimination of the last error.

There is another bugaboo in the traditional method of predicting rate of gain from practice from a measure of initial ability. This is the fact of correlation of errors of measurement. Since gain is defined as the difference between final ability and initial ability, the correlation between gain and initial ability will be lowered by the fact that errors of measurement are negatively correlated. Thus, if Subject A gets an obtained score on Trial 1 that is higher than his true score, the measure of gain will be spuriously low.

By way of summary, let me repeat that the difficulties in using traditional definitions of learning ability are: 1) the fact that subjects enter the experiment with differing amounts of prior practice, 2) the lack of an absolute zero point, 3) the lack of true units, and 4) the negative correlation of errors of measurement. A method must be found which overcomes or avoids these difficulties. There is a method which appears to do this. This method makes use of common points of mastery and has two variants. It also has one innovator and two users. The innovator was E. L. Thorndike, who first described the method in his book, *Adult Learning* (1928). I also have applied the method to several sets of data, which I will describe here today.

As I have said, the initial steps in treating the raw data are the same for both variants. The learning curves based on the trial scores for each subject are smoothed by a running average covering enough points to eliminate serious chance fluctuations in the scores. After all of the individual records are smoothed in this fashion an initial common point of mastery is selected. That is to say, a particular level of performance common to the early trials of all subjects is determined by inspection. From this point on the procedure varies according to which of the two common point methods is used.

In Method A a second or final common point of mastery is selected. This point must also be common to the curves of all subjects. Learning ability is then defined as the number of trials or the number of errors or the amount of time required to improve from the initial to the final common point of mastery. It should be noticed that this definition of learning ability is free from the objections raised against the two traditional definitions. All subjects pass through the same range of performance. They all start at the same point. The only assumption which need be made here is that ten trials represent more effort than nine trials.

In Method B the initial common point of mastery is established in the manner just described, and learning ability is defined as the amount of improvement in the first segment of trials beyond this common point. The length of the segment employed will be constant for all subjects and will depend upon the statistical reliability of the data. It will be seen that with Method B all subjects start at the same point of mastery and the difficulties encountered when initial performance varies from subject to subject or from group to group are thus obviated.

Two problems of major significance in the psychology of learning have been attacked with this methodology. The results in both instances are gratifying if they are to be regarded as typical of all results to follow.

The first problem studied was that of the relationship between initial learning ability and physiological limit. A search of the literature revealed three long-time training experiments for which the individual subject's records by trial were available. These groups of published data have been analyzed by the common point method.

The first of these groups was from an experiment conducted in which ten subjects practiced addition five minutes per day for 30 days consecutively except for Sundays (Wells, 1913). Of the original ten subjects only eight could be used, as the other two did not show sufficient overlapping. This number is too small to have any real significance, but since the results of this analysis are consistent with those based on larger groups, they are included in this report.

The second group of data was composed of the individual records of 15 subjects who practiced the three-hole coordination test in connection with Hollingworth's experiment on the effects of caffeine (1912). Each subject made 500 touches in a practice period and there were 26 of the practice periods. The scores used were the time required for 500 touches. These data are given in the appendix of Thorndike's *Adult*

Learning. It was necessary to omit one subject who did not show a common point.

The third and largest group of subjects was those of Chapman's experiment on learning to typewrite (1919). The 19 subjects who completed at least 154 hours of practice were included in this analysis. The analysis of the Chapman data is especially interesting because of the practical importance of accurate prediction of final ability in typing. Moreover, the number of cases was greater than in the other two experiments and the total amount of practice was greater. It must be pointed out that the subjects in the Chapman experiment had not yet reached their physiological limits but had probably reached a point beyond which no further crisscrossing of the learning curves would occur. The subjects were tested every second hour by means of five-minute tests. These test scores are the data analyzed in this study. Since certain subjects missed some of the tests, it was necessary to interpolate. This was done before the curves were smoothed.

All curves were smoothed by a running average covering ten points. Thus each point on the curves after smoothing represented about 50 minutes of testing in the case of each of the three groups. With tests of this length statistical reliability may be assumed.

It was found that the common point method predicts final ability better than the traditional method does. This finding was true for the Wells data, the Hollingworth data, and the Chapman data. Interestingly enough, the common point method shows higher prediction than the traditional method even though the traditional method is based on a larger number of trials. In the case of the Wells data on learning addition, the common point method yielded a predictive coefficient of .99, as against .81 for the traditional. In the case of the Hollingworth data on learning the three-hole coordination task, the predictive coefficient for the common point method was .80, as against .38 for the traditional method. In the case of the Chapman data on learning to typewrite, the subjects had not yet reached their physiological limit, but here again the common point method was superior, showing a predictive coefficient of .63 as against .39 for the traditional method.

A preliminary investigation which, to the best of my knowledge, has not been repeated with other data during the past 30 years indicates that the method of common points of mastery might have considerable promise in the study of the intercorrelations between learning ability for different tasks. In Hollingworth's original experiment, the 16 subjects learned three tasks. These were the three-hole coordination task, opposites, and arithmetic calculation. In the opposites test, performance was scored as the amount of time required to name 250 opposites. The data were smoothed, as before, by means of a running average. When the learning ability score based on the common point of mastery was computed, it was found to be .59. Several variants of the traditional method of measuring learning ability were employed. One of these employed the difference between the first and fourth blocks of five trials and yielded an intercorrelation of −.14. Another calculation made use of the difference between the first and second blocks of five trials and yielded an intercorrelation of −.17. The intercorrelation based upon the difference between the third and fourth blocks of five trials was −.11.

In an attempt to explain the higher correlations obtained with the common point method as compared to the traditional method, I will repeat, or at least rephrase, some of the points made at the opening of this paper.

To make the explanation simple, let us assume that there *is* a correlation between innate learning ability and physiological limit or between innate ability to learn two different tasks. In the typical learning experiment the subjects are far from unpracticed at the moment the conditions of a formal learning experiment are imposed upon them. They have already had some opportunity to practice the skill in question. How much haphazard practice they have had is not on the record. What we know definitely is that subjects show individual differences in performance on the very first trial of the formal experiment. One subject might have a high initial status because he has had much unrecorded prior practice though he may be only average in native learning capacity. Another subject might make a low initial score because he is average in native capacity and has had but a small amount of prior practice. A third subject might stand high on the first trial by virtue of great native capacity even though he has had little unrecorded prior practice. These are just a few of the combinations of prior practice, native capacity, and initial performance. Add to this motley of variable unknowns the further fact that absolute gains have different meanings in terms of ability at different ranges of the scale and it would appear that in the traditional method we are dealing with enough attenuating and distorting factors to conceal a fairly sizeable correlation. The method of common points eliminates variable initial ability and allows gain to be determined systematically by native capacity beyond that point.

In conclusion, let me express the hope that some of you will have access to data on a larger number of tasks and a larger number of subjects learning over longer periods of time and will have the interest to apply to these data the method I have described to you. If you have the data but not the interest, I would be very happy to receive a copy of the data and do the analysis myself.

The Relation Between Two Measures of Learning: Residual Gain and Common Points of Mastery

Ronald P. Carver

American Institutes for Research

[Since the procedures described by Ruch in the preceding paper appear to accomplish much the same objective in the measurement of learning as that accomplished by the residual gain procedure, Carver felt that it would be interesting to apply the two procedures to the same data and compare the results obtained. Despite several problems that were encountered in the implementation of the idea, the comparison of the two approaches to measuring gain, and the relationship of these measures to other variables, are of considerable interest.]

This is an investigation of the relationship between the common points of mastery and the residual gain methods of measuring learning. Both purport to overcome or avoid a number of difficulties of the traditional methods. One of the difficulties is that subjects often enter the learning situation with differing amounts of prior practice. Gain measures which fail to take these differences into account are penalizing subjects who are high on a negatively accelerated learning curve, since those low on the learning curve are in the phase of rapid acceleration. This disadvantage might be overcome by using a starting point which is common to all subjects when the common points of mastery measure is used. The residual gain measure is said to overcome this difficulty by virtue of its zero correlation with initial score. Another difficulty involved in measuring gain is the lack of an absolute zero in measurement. A gain measure which assumes a zero point, such as per cent gain, when the assumption is definitely not warranted, must be regarded as exceedingly crude. Both residual gain and common points of mastery claim to be pertinent to the measurement of gain without the assumption of a zero point of measurement. Finally, there is the preponderant difficulty of units of measurement. Does a gain at one end of the measurement scale reflect the same amount of what one is seeking to measure as a numerically equivalent gain at the other end of the scale? Again, by virtue of the particular technique, both measures claim to overcome this difficulty. And Ruch (1936) claims the additional advantage of being able to overcome the negative correlation of the errors of measurement with common points of mastery.

In view of the many advantages attributed to the two methods of measuring gain, it seemed desirable to conduct an investigation of the relationship between them. Also to be investigated was the relationship between each of the two gain variables and other known variables.

Gain in a learning experiment or learning task is normally defined as learning. It was hypothesized that there would be a significant correlation between these two measures of gain, since both measures purport to measure the same general quality.

Considering the currently purported positive relation between learning and intelligence (Wallen, 1962) it was hypothesized that there would be a significant correlation between each of these measures and verbal intelligence. This hypothesis was advanced even though past research, reviewed by Woodrow (1946), which used various gain measures as measures of learning, failed to find a significant correlation between learning and intelligence.

Conversely, it was hypothesized that aptitude scores, such as measures of numerical and mechanical ability, would not be significantly correlated with either of the measures of gain.

SUBJECTS

The subjects were 874 US Navy enlisted men in the lowest two pay grades. In general, they had graduated from high school during the previous year. They were awaiting entry into one of the technical training schools at the Naval Air Technical Training Center, Millington, Tennessee.

TESTS

The learning test used was the DuBois-Bunch Learning Test (Du-Bois and Bunch, 1949). This is a simple perceptual learning task, in which the task is to identify a subpattern which is repeated within a larger pattern containing four subpatterns. Answers are indicated on standard IBM five-choice answer sheets; one choice is assigned to each of the four subpatterns and the fifth is assigned to the category wherein none of the subpatterns is repeated. Each trial consists of 30 items and the total test contains ten such trials. The test was administered by using 90-second trials and a 30-second rest pause between trials.

The Navy General Classification Test (GCT) was used as a measure of verbal intelligence. This test was designed to measure verbal ability, testing the comprehension of word meaning and verbal relationships.

Designed to measure skills in fundamental arithmetic processes, arithmetic reasoning, and problem solving, the Navy Arithmetic Test (ARI) was used as a measure of numerical aptitude.

The Navy Mechanical Test (MECH) was used to test mechanical aptitude. It was designed to measure comprehension of mechanical principles and basic mechanical knowledge.

DATA ANALYSIS

The common points of mastery variable was developed through the following steps:

1. Each pair of the ten adjacent trial scores (number right for the trial) was summed for each subject thus giving nine sum scores for each subject.

2. A frequency distribution was obtained for each of the nine sum scores.

3. The mean of each of the nine sum scores was computed.

4. The above frequency distribution and means were inspected and then 16 pairs of lower and upper sum points were selected. To increase the number of subjects that might have a pair of sum points, each upper and lower point was in effect a multiple point since each point was represented by two scores. The lowest of the upper sum points (24, 25) was selected approximately midway between the mean of the initial sum (18.8) and the mean of the final sum (27.6). The remainder of the upper sum points were selected in successively ascending order (26,27: 28,29: 30,31) to a point beyond which an adequate number of subjects, who would have both that particular upper sum point and also a lower sum point, seemed doubtful. The lower sum points (16,17: 18,19: 20,21: and 22,23) were selected in a similar manner descending from the lowest of the upper sum points. The final 16 pairs of lower and upper sum points were then all combinations of the four upper sum points and the four lower sum points.

5. The number of trials needed to progress from the lower sum point to the upper sum point was obtained for each subject, whose results contained both of the above lower and upper points that made a pair.

The summing of two adjacent scores in Step 1 above was done to approximate Ruch's (1936) suggested smoothing procedure and to make the data more stable. Steps 2 and 3 were adopted in order to facilitate the choosing of an appropriate pair of lower and upper sum points. Since there is no definite criterion as to what constitutes a good lower or upper sum point, 16 different pairs of points were chosen in Step 4. Step 5 gave the desired variable and was symbolized by C for common points of mastery score.

The correlation of residual gain with common points of mastery was accomplished in the following manner:

1. The intercorrelations of the initial sum score (I), the final sum score (F), and the common points of mastery score (C) were computed.

2. The part correlational formula, below, was used to compute the desired correlation.

$$r_{(F.I)C} = \frac{r_{FC} - r_{IF}r_{IC}}{\sqrt{1 - r_{IF}^2}}$$

RESULTS

The mean of each of the nine sum scores for the entire sample (N = 874) is shown in Figure 16. Notice that there was a definite increase or gain as the number of trials increased. The mean of the initial sum (I) was 18.8 and the mean of the final sum (F) was 27.6.

The correlation between the initial sum (I) and the final sum (F) for the entire sample was .69 (r_{IF}). The correlation between the two trial scores (Trials 1 and 2) that were summed to get the initial sum (I) was .67, and the corresponding correlation between Trials 9 and 10 for the final sum (F) was .77. When the two preceding correlations were used to estimate the reliability of the initial and final sum scores, they were found to be .80 and .87, respectively. Using the correlation between the initial and final sum scores (.69), together with their respective estimates of reliability, in the appropriate formula (Manning and DuBois, 1962) an estimate of the reliability of the residual gain score for the entire sample was .59.

The correlation of residual gain (F.I) with common points of mastery (C) for each of 16 different pairs of lower and upper points is shown in Table 6. The significance, as well as the number in each group (N) for each of the correlations, is also presented. Notice that, with only one exception, all of the seven significant correlations involve lower

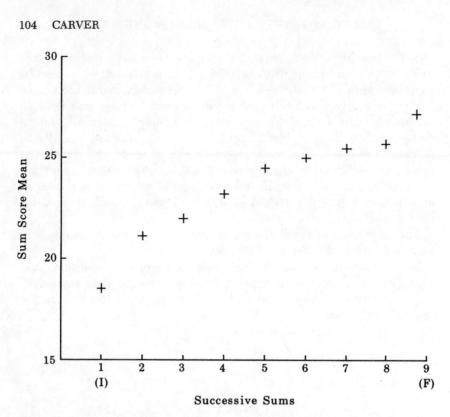

Figure 16. Sum Score Means on DuBois-Bunch Learning Test

points and upper points that are between the means of the initial (I) and the final (F) sum scores.

DISCUSSION

It can be seen from the correlations in Table 6 that there is a significant correlation between residual gain and common points of mastery when the common points lie between the means of the initial and final scores used for the computation of the residual gain score.

The procedures advanced by Ruch (1936) for locating the common points make it highly unlikely that the lower common point would be located below the mean of the initial score or higher than the mean of the final score. Therefore, the results were interpreted as supporting the hypothesis that there is a significant correlation between these two gain measures.

Although significant, the correlation between these two measures was very low. The highest correlation was .27. However, no attempt

Table 6

CORRELATIONS BETWEEN RESIDUAL GAIN AND
COMMON POINTS OF MASTERY

| | | Lower Common Point | | | |
		16,17	18,19	20,21	22,23
	30,31	.10	.08	.07	.04
		N = 29	N = 79	N = 102	N = 141
Upper Common Point	28,29	−.04	.11	.13	.15*
		N = 34	N = 113	N = 169	N = 203
	26,27	.11	.22**	.19**	.27***
		N = 95	N = 156	N = 213	N = 259
	24,25	.11	.21**	.17**	.13*
		N = 118	N = 183	N = 227	N = 251

*Significant at 0.05 level
**Significant at 0.01 level
***Significant at 0.001 level

was made in this investigation to correct these correlations for attenuation.

The summing procedure used in this investigation was an attempt to approach the smoothing of the learning curves as prescribed by Ruch to increase the reliability of the common points of mastery score. However, the summing procedure undoubtedly does not reach the smoothness desired by Ruch, and thereby decreases the reliability of this gain measure. Also, the number of scores used, nine, in this investigation restricted the range of this gain measure so that it only varied from one to eight. The reliability of the common points of mastery score was therefore low.

The reliability of the residual gain measure estimated for the entire N of 874 was only .59.

In this investigation it was established that there was a definite relationship between the two measures of gain, residual gain and common points of mastery. However, the degree of this relationship was very low. It was, nevertheless, speculated that the unreliability of the two measures was concealing a fairly sizeable correlation.

None of the correlations of either gain measure with verbal intelligence (GCT) or with the two aptitude measures (ARI and MECH) was significant.

The hypothesis that there was a significant correlation between learning and verbal intelligence, as they have been measured in this study, could not be supported. This result is somewhat contrary to the relationship reported by Wallen (1962). It is similar to the earlier research reviewed by Woodrow (1946) where no significant relationship was found between learning and intelligence when the measurement of learning was restricted to a gain measure rather than an achievement measure.

This research then failed to support the purported positive relation between learning and intelligence, since the null hypothesis could not be rejected.

As previously stated, the learning task in this study was a simple perceptual learning task. Any interpretation of the failure of this study to find a significant relationship between learning and either verbal intelligence or aptitude, should take the nature of the learning task into account.

PART III

Method and Results

As emphasized in the introduction to Part II, educational evaluation is not complete until quantitative information is applied in the type of environment from which the original observations came. Similarly, a treatise which considers basic issues in training research and various aspects of the measurement of learning is incomplete until it brings the earlier points to meaningful fruition. This should take the form of methods that have not only been formulated in detail but have been found to make a worthwhile contribution in the real world of educational evaluation. This final section undertakes to do this in the framework of the Washington University–Office of Naval Research project on research strategies for evaluating training. The products described are three strategies or experimental designs that have been tried a number of times in various facets of educational evaluation and have achieved some degree of success. None of the methods described makes any claim to being new. It is more a matter of further development, extension, or adaptation than of novel discovery.

Evaluation of an educational program is a broader undertaking than is measurement of learning in such a program. But few would deny that the amount learned is one of the best indicia of the excellence of an educational program. In practical terms, when we speak of measurement of learning we are referring to change which comes about as a result of tuition. Observation of practical educational programs confirm, however, that we seldom attempt to measure change. As a rule, we measure current status. If student A scores higher on a mid-term test than student B, we often infer that he has learned more than student B. It is quite possible that student B began the course farther below student A than was the case at the time of the midterm test, and hence learned more during the first half of the course than did student A. This is not an improbable, isolated possibility, but instead occurs with considerable frequency. From the standpoint of knowledge students have concerning the material presented, the scores may be adequate, but in terms of the effectiveness of the educational program, little can be inferred without taking into account the change in knowledge that occurred between the time the students started the course and the time the midterm test was taken.

The above rationale, while seldom taken into account in educational and training situations, often has been recognized in research studies. More often than not, however, researchers have done the obvious (subtracted initial status from status following tuition) and have thereby fallen into a not quite so obvious trap. There is a systematic tendency for the gains of students with low initial status to exceed those of students with high initial status. Under certain conditions this can result in misleading data. For development of this point and a proposed remedy see DuBois' paper, which is the initial paper in this section of the monograph. Three other papers in this section report on the application of the method to practical or theoretical problems of educational evaluation.

Correlational Analysis in Training Research

Philip H. DuBois

Washington University

[This is the first of three papers which describe a fully developed procedure for use in educational and training research. The multivariate correlational procedures described in this paper have been the focal point for a large part of the work that has been accomplished under the contract. In this paper DuBois describes the objectional characteristics of a gain score which is simply the difference between a pretest score and an endtest score. This measure of gain is referred to as crude gain. He then goes on to show that most of the objections to crude gain can be overcome through the appropriate use of a long known but almost forgotten statistic, part correlation. The gain score resulting when this statistical procedure is used is referred to as residual gain. In the absence of some sort of clearly superior criterion, which does not exist, it is difficult to demonstrate empirically the superiority of residual gain over crude gain. But considerable suggestive data, statistical consistency, and logical argument are offered in support of the use of residual gain in the study of correlates of learning.]

In practical training situations a question of considerable interest is the determination of the correlates of learning. With what factors are student gains associated? Are factors within the student, such as aptitudes and interests, more important than factors within the training situation, such as personal characteristics of instructors, the use of training aids and the introduction of incentives? It is obvious that there can be no one answer that is universally true. In some training situations, variance associated with the student is undoubtedly more important than variance associated with the instructor. In other cases, such as instances in which the students are relatively homogeneous as to ability and motivation, the reverse may be true. However, if we wish to be able to generalize about the relative importance of factors in complex training situations, methods of making appropriate statistical analyses are required.

When an individual learns a new skill or masters a new subject, he always builds upon existing abilities or information. Never does he start from zero even when, for example, he is being trained in a language with which he is totally unfamiliar. His years of experience in the manipulation of verbal symbols influence his acquisition of a new set of verbal symbols. In all studies of human learning, even in new and apparently unfamiliar psychomotor tasks, there is undoubtedly considerable variability with respect to initial status, resulting in part from differences in previous experiences.

In the analysis of learning it is often assumed that our measurements are in terms of ratio scales, that is, scales with known zero points. Such an assumption is not necessary. As long as we are measuring with interval scales, in which the units are additive, we can analyze learning by applying correlational techniques.

Estimates of per cent gain assume that the researcher is using a ratio scale. It may be pointed out, however, that the use of scales with additive units and known zero points, such as errors or seconds or units of work accomplished, does not necessarily guarantee that differences between initial and final status constitute meaningful variables that can be used in investigations of conditions influencing learning. The trouble with a crude difference score is that it is a mere positive weighting of final score and negative weighting of initial score with effective weights completely unknown. Its correlations with variables describing the learners and defining the external conditions of the study are greatly influenced by the vagaries of its composition. That crude gain will correlate negatively with initial status is practically certain.

Let x_1 be initial score, x_2 be final score, and x_g be the gain. Then,

$$x_g = x_2 - x_1$$

Multiplying by x_1,

$$x_1 x_g = x_1 x_2 - x_1^2$$

Summing, dividing by N and writing equivalents,

$$r_{1g} s_1 s_g = r_{12} s_1 s_2 - s_1^2$$

Since s's are always positive, for r_{1g} to be positive it is necessary that

$$r_{12}s_2 > s_1 \tag{1}$$

If r_{12} is .00 or negative, the condition stated in (1) cannot be fulfilled. If r_{12} is positive, the following minimum ratios must hold for r_{1g} to be positive:

r_{12}	s_2/s_1
.10	10.00
.20	5.00
.30	3.33
.40	2.50
.50	2.00
.60	1.67
.70	1.43
.80	1.25
.90	1.11

In the vast majority of learning studies, it will therefore be found that the correlation between initial score and crude gain is negative.

Let us consider two points in time at which we have adequate and reliable measures of some aspect of behavior. Let z_1 be our first measure in z-score form and z_2 our second measure. We can divide z_2 into two uncorrelated portions: $\tilde{z}_2$, which correlates perfectly with z_1 and $z_{2.1}$, which is uncorrelated with z_1. In the conventional formula for a zero order regression equation, $\tilde{z}_2 = r_{12}z_1$.

Accordingly,

$$z_2 - \tilde{z}_2 = z_2 - r_{12}z_1 = z_{2.1} \tag{2}$$

All change in function is included in this residual score, which may be taken as reflecting learning or gain. The absolute magnitude of the residual score is of no direct interest, as we are interested only in its correlations.

It is proposed that in learning situations in which all subjects do not start at a common point that this residual, $z_{2.1}$, be used as the measure of change. The use of a residual score to define change has several advantages:

1. It can be defined precisely and meaningfully.

2. The residual in z-form is completely independent of units of measurement and hence is applicable even if initial score and final score are in different metrics.

3. The residual is completely independent of and completely uncorrelated with initial status. Hence when it is correlated with outside

variables, correlation is with gain defined as independent of initial status, rather than a mixed function, an unknown part of which is initial status.

4. The residual does not require the use of a ratio scale to measure initial and final status. By the use of a residual score the question as to whether those who know most at the start of the study learn more than the others cannot be answered, since the answer to such a question would depend on the use of the same ratio scale at the beginning and end of the study. However, there is no restriction on investigations of outside correlates of learning.

5. The residual score as a measure of learning fits perfectly into correlational statistics in terms of variances. The variance of the final score is divisible into two uncorrelated portions: a part associated with and a part independent of initial status. The independent part can in turn be analyzed to find proportions associated with outside predictors of learning. These analyses should help us understand what goes on during the learning process.

6. While only first order residuals are considered here, it is perfectly feasible statistically to use residuals of any order as measures of learning, thus dissociating gain from any number of variables known to be associated with final status.

The correlation between a residual score, $z_{2.1}$, and a third variable, z_3, is given by the formula.

$$r_{(2.1)3} = \frac{r_{23} - r_{12}r_{13}}{\sqrt{1 - r_{12}^2}} \qquad (3)$$

This is a first order part correlation as described by Franzen (1928). It is applicable to correlating change in function, defined as measured later status less that part of the variance associated with earlier status, with any third variable.

The correlation between two sets of residual scores, $z_{2.1}$ and $z_{4.3}$, may be found from the formula:

$$r_{(2.1)(4.3)} = \frac{r_{24} - r_{12}r_{14} - r_{23}r_{34} + r_{12}r_{13}r_{34}}{\sqrt{1 - r_{12}^2} \ \sqrt{1 - r_{34}^2}} \qquad (4)$$

This formula is also given by Franzen and is appropriate for finding the intercorrelations of gains in different learning tasks.

The multiple correlation between a residual score and any combination of outside variables, whether referring to measured characteristics of trainees or to characteristics of instructors or to experimental conditions, may be readily obtained. The first step is to correlate the gain with each outside variable by means of Formula 3. The second step is to compute the multiple correlation between the outside variables as predictors and $z_{2.1}$ as the criterion by any of the ordinary methods for computing multiple R.

It is not to be supposed that the residual score is a pure measure of change. Its usefulness depends upon the degree to which z_1 validly and reliably measures initial status and the degree to which z_2 validly and reliably measures final status. If nonpertinent variance is introduced into one of the measures but not the other, r_{12} will be reduced and $z_{2.1}$ will be too large.

Like any difference between positively correlated scores, the reliability of a residual tends to be somewhat lower than the reliabilities of its components. We correlate the residual $(z_2 - r_{12}z_1)$ with its theoretical equivalent $(z'_2 - r'_{12}z'_1)$. It is assumed that all correlations between an initial score and a final score equal r_{12}. The reliabilities of the initial score and final score are, respectively, r_{11} and r_{22}. Then

$$r_{(2.1)(2.1)} = \frac{r_{22} - r_{12}^2 \ (2 - r_{11})}{1 - r_{12}^2} \tag{5}$$

Data which illustrate the application of part correlation in a practical training situation have been supplied by Dr. Curtis Trainer and are summarized in Table 7. In each phase of training, Trainer used alternate forms of the same proficiency test as measures of initial and final status. Crude gain was simply score on the final test less the score on

Table 7

PREDICTION OF GAIN

Comparison of correlations between electrical aptitude index and crude gain and residual score, together with correlations between initial test and crude gain. Data for four phases of Ground Radio Mechanics School and five phases of Airborne Radio Mechanics School supplied by Curtis L. Trainer of the 3300th Training Publications Unit of Air Training Command.

Phase of Training	N	(1)	(2)	(3)
Ground—Phase 1	187	.29	.42	−.33
Ground—Phase 2	187	.42	.48	−.18
Ground—Phase 3	187	.34	.43	−.30
Ground—Phase 4	187	.26	.34	−.25
Airborne—Phase 1	376	.40	.46	−.19
Airborne—Phase 2	254	.46	.48	−.24
Airborne—Phase 3	295	.36	.47	−.34
Airborne—Phase 4	319	.37	.46	−.48
Airborne—Phase 5	251	.26	.30	−.26

(1) Correlation between electrical aptitude index and crude gain.
(2) Part correlation between electrical aptitude index and final test less variance associated with initial test.
(3) Correlation between initial test and crude gain.

the pretest. Correlations with residual score were computed by means of Formula 3. In Column 3 it will be noted that the correlation between initial score and crude gain is negative in the four phases of Ground Radio Mechanics School and in five phases of Airborne Radio Mechanics School. When Electrical Aptitude Index is used as a predictor, correlations with residual score are higher than with crude gain.

There is no direct information from these correlations as to whether crude gain or the residual score is the better measure of learning. However, we can state that the correlation of an outside variable with a residual score may be quite different from the correlation with a crude gain score.

Table 8 provides evidence that residual gains from different tasks have somewhat higher and somewhat more consistent intercorrelations than do crude gains scores.

Table 8

INTERCORRELATIONS OF LEARNING SCORES

Intercorrelations of crude gains scores as reported by Roff, Payne, and Moore (1954) above the diagonal; intercorrelations of residual scores by Formula 4 below the diagonal. N = 175 USAF Airmen.

Variable	1	2	3
1		.11	.16
2	.21		.19
3	.19	.24	

All variables based upon first 3 and last 3 trials of a total of 40 trials on the following psychomotor tests: 1. Complex Coordination Test; 2. Multidimensional Pursuit Test; 3. Rotary Pursuit Test.

A further problem in the correlational analysis of training is the determination of whether change in the earlier parts of the learning process is more predictable than change in the latter parts. It is suggested that there are two ways of treating this problem. The first is by a cumulative system.

Consider a learning situation in which there are four points in time, 1, 2, 3, and 4, at which proficiency is measured. From these four measures we can derive three residuals, $z_{2.1}$, $z_{3.1}$ and $z_{4.1}$. They are not mutually exclusive since $z_{3.1}$ includes $z_{2.1}$, and $z_{4.1}$ includes $z_{3.1}$. Intercorrelations of these residuals would be partial r's. When these residuals are correlated with outside predictors we can compare the degree to which gains can be predicted over varying lengths of training time. Such correlations are part correlations.

A second type of analysis consists in dividing the total gain into $(n - 1)$ uncorrelated portions, which with four measured points, would be $z_{2.1}$, $z_{3.12}$, and $z_{4.123}$. These again are residuals. The variance at z_2

less the variance predictable from z_1 is $z_{2.1}$; $z_{3.12}$ is the variance at z_3 less the variance predictable from z_1 and z_2, while $z_{4.123}$ is the variance at z_4 less the variance predictable from z_1, z_2 and z_3. When we correlate outside variables with $z_{2.1}$ we investigate the correlates of change during the initial period. When we correlate outside variables with $z_{3.12}$ we investigate the correlates of the part of the overall change which is independent of the change during the initial period, and so on.

The correlation of an outside variable with $z_{3.12}$ is a second order part correlation, the correlation with $z_{4.123}$ is a third order part correlation, and so on. Numerically, these part correlations are always a little lower than corresponding partial correlations.

A numerical example is shown in Table 9. Here we have measurements at only three points on the curve. However, the data indicate that gain during the first half is more predictable than overall gain. Gain during the second half defined as independent of gain during the first half is the least predictable of the three learning measures.

SUMMARY

In investigations of learning, especially in complex training situations where learners enter into an investigative study with different degrees

Table 9

PREDICTION OF LEARNING BY PERIODS

Training was on three psychomotor tests (Rotary Pursuit, Multidimensional Pursuit, and Complex Coordination). Original scores were: sum of first three trials (1), sum of middle three trials (2), and sum of last three trials (3). Predictors are three tests from the USAF Airmen's Battery (Electrical Information, Memory for Landmarks, and Pattern Comprehension). All correlations are multiple R's. Original correlations reported by Roff, Payne, and Moore (1954). $N = 175$.

	Rotary Pursuit	Multidimensional Pursuit	Complex Coordination
$R_{(3.1)x}$	.24	.11	.15
$R_{(2.1)x}$	.24	.19	.22
$R_{(3.2)x}$	.12	.08	.17

$R_{(3.1)x}$ is the multiple correlation between the battery of predictors and change during the entire training period.

$R_{(2.1)x}$ is the multiple correlation between the battery of predictors and change during the first half of the training period.

$R_{(3.2)x}$ is the multiple correlation between the battery of predictors and change during the second half of the training period.

of the skill or knowledge, it appears that an appropriate tool of analysis is part correlation. Logically, we divide the measured variance in skill or knowledge at some point into two parts: a part which is completely predicted from the measured skill or knowledge at some earlier point and a part which is unpredicted from the earlier measure. This residual is then correlated with outside predictors of learning, either singly or in a multiple regression equation.

If desired, variance associated with any number of variables can be removed from the residual prior to correlating it with outside predictors. In this way it is possible to control statistically factors such as amount of previous training, age, experience in a specialty, and the like.

The numerical examples in and of themselves cannot reveal whether the present method of analyzing training gains is better than analyzing crude gain. However, the numerical examples show that: (1) crude gain is consistently correlated negatively with initial status, (2) the correlations of residual gain are more consistent and more in line with what might be logically expected than are the correlations of crude gains, and (3) residual measures of learning seem to have more in common than do measures of crude gain in the same functions.

It appears, therefore, that the method of residual gain, or, if you prefer, the method of part correlation is a promising means of investigating learning in complex training situations.

Analysis of Covariance in Training Research

David Bakan
York University

[Bakan's paper describes the second of the three methods referred to in the introduction to this part of the monograph. In common with the other two, Bakan is thinking in terms of a method that is applicable to an ongoing educational situation, one in which the use of rigorous experimental controls may not be practicable. He deftly singles out the aspects of covariance procedures that are pertinent to applied educational research, pointing out just what is taking place at each point in the procedure and how the results may be interpreted.

At the conference at which Bakan's paper was presented, it was followed by an extended discussion of the similarities and differences between covariance procedures on the one hand and partial and part correlation procedures as described earlier by DuBois on the other.

It was agreed that when applied to essentially the same problem, the two methods should give virtually the same results. The choice between the methods should be based primarily upon whether the question one wishes to answer can be couched better in the covariance framework or in the residual gain framework.]

It is the purpose of this paper to outline some of the features of analysis of covariance as a device for studying the varying effects of different training procedures. The paper is offered with the suggestion that the method has potentialities which far exceed its exploitation up to the present time. We will leave out of consideration the calculational details, which are readily available in many places.

THE EXPERIMENTAL PARADIGM

The experimental paradigm to which all of the subsequent discussion refers is one which is often satisfied in training studies. We consider a class of subjects who have been subdivided into different groups, each of which will be subjected to a different procedure of training. We consider, furthermore, the situation in which, perhaps because of administrative difficulties, the assignment of the subjects has been made without the fulfillment of a randomizing procedure, such that, perhaps, the means of the group on some measure, X, which is presumably the measure of the subjects' initial competence, vary significantly at the outset.

When our groups have gone through these different training procedures, we take a single test which provides a measure Y, and which presumably reflects the competence of the subjects after training. The paradigm does not require that X and Y shall be measures of the same class. For example, X could be pencil and paper test and Y an on-the-job performance measure, or they could be any other pair of measures which are thought to be relevant.

Although the paradigm does not require it, the experiment will be trivialized if either of the following conditions prevails:

1. If the correlation between X and Y is perfect. In this instance the variation among Y-scores would be completely the result of the variation among the X-scores, and in effect the different methods of training would be completely a matter of indifference.

2. If the correlation between X and Y is zero. In this case there would be no additional value in using the X-measure, since it is unrelated to the Y-score.

If either of these conditions prevails, the analysis of covariance will reveal it. In the first instance the ultimate test of the corrected Y-means would be the same as for the X-means. In the second instance the ultimate test of the corrected Y-means would be the same as the test of uncorrected Y-means.

The ideal condition for the application of analysis of covariance is where the correlation between X and Y is substantial, but neither .00 nor 1.00. In terms of our understanding of most training studies, the Y-score is usually *partly* determined by the initial level of competence of the subjects, as shown by the X-score, and *partly* determined by the training methods. The objective of the analysis is to extract and separate each of the effects. When we talk of corrected Y-means, we mean Y-means with the effect of X removed.

For the sake of simplicity we will restrict our discussion to the problem where the only control variable outside of the groups will be X. However, analysis of covariance can be used where there are other control variables analogous to X and to more than a single classification of Y-scores.

THE ESSENTIAL PARTITIONING IN ANALYSIS OF COVARIANCE

In the analysis of covariance there are three major partitionings of the variation and correlation among the data:

1. There is first the simple division of the X and Y sum of squares and degrees of freedom into Between Groups and Within Groups.

2. In addition to this, that which is a function of both the X and Y, the sums of the products of their deviations from the mean, SSxy, is also divisible into two components, such that we have a sum of cross products Between Groups and a sum of cross products Within Groups. The Within Groups SSxy is based on deviations from group means. The Between Groups SSx and SSy are based on the deviation of group means from grand means.

3. The final essential partitioning is the result of the action of both variables. This is a second breakdown of SSy into the sum of squares for regression plus the sum of squares of deviations from regression. In the usual analysis of covariance this is done twice: once on the Within Group SSy and once on the Total SSy.

THE RELATIONSHIP OF (SSy = SS REG. + SS DEV. FROM REGRESSION) TO CORRELATION

Before showing its application to the remainder of analysis of covariance, let us attempt to elucidate the nature of the last breakdown mentioned above.

If we write the breakdown in deviation form, we have

$$\Sigma y^2 = \frac{(\Sigma xy)^2}{\Sigma x^2} + \left(\Sigma y^2 - \frac{(\Sigma xy)^2}{\Sigma x^2} \right) \tag{1}$$

If we consider that the original number of degrees of freedom is n, and the number of degrees of freedom associated with Σy^2 is $(n-1)$, then we can set up the following table, allowing 1 degree of freedom for the regression.

Source	SS	df.
Regression	$\dfrac{(\Sigma xy)^2}{\Sigma x^2}$	1
Dev. from reg.	$\Sigma y^2 - \dfrac{(\Sigma xy)^2}{\Sigma x^2}$	$(n-2)$
Total	Σy^2	$(n-1)$

$$(2)$$

We then note that the adequate[1] test of the regression is:

$$F = \frac{\dfrac{(\Sigma xy)^2}{\Sigma x^2}}{\Sigma y^2 - \dfrac{(\Sigma xy)^2}{\Sigma x^2}} \ (n-2) \tag{3}$$

which becomes:

$$F = \frac{\dfrac{(\Sigma xy)^2}{\Sigma x^2 \Sigma y^2}}{1 - \dfrac{(\Sigma xy)^2}{\Sigma x^2 \Sigma y^2}} \ (n-2) \tag{4}$$

$$F = \frac{r^2}{1 - r^2} \ (n-2) \tag{5}$$

or, taking advantage of the fact that, when there is 1 degree of freedom in the numerator, $F = t^2$,

$$t = r \sqrt{(n-2)/(1-r^2)} \tag{6}$$

which is exactly the usual test for the significance of a correlation co-efficient.

The application of the F test provides us immediately with the possibility of testing not only the correlation between X and Y for all the scores, but gives us a separate test of the significance of the correlation within groups, effectively removing any effects associated either with the mean of X or the mean of Y.

Aside from all other considerations, if there should be any effect on the correlation due to the relationship among the means, this latter test provides us with what is, in some sense, a purer picture of the association of X and Y.

---

[1] This paper was written by the author before the publication of Bakan, D., "The test of significance in psychological research" (*Psychological Bulletin*, 1966, 66, 423-437). Some of the considerations in that paper would suggest that the test of significance here should be interpreted more as descriptive than inferential, at the very least.

THE DIRECT APPLICATION OF (SSy = SS REG. + SS DEV. FROM REGRESSION)

In actual use in analysis of covariance the formula is modified to the form

$$\text{SS dev. from regression} = \text{SSy} - \text{SS reg.} \tag{7}$$

or

$$\text{SS}'\text{y} = \text{SSy} - \text{SS reg. for simplicity of notation.} \tag{8}$$

The ultimate test is made based upon SS'y. Earlier it was indicated that neither a perfect nor a zero correlation is very suitable for analysis of covariance. If the correlation is perfect then

$$\text{SS}'\text{y} = \text{SS reg.} \tag{9}$$

and if the correlation is zero then

$$\text{SS}'\text{y} = \text{SSy} \tag{10}$$

In the first case the test resolves itself into a test of X, and in the latter no advantage has been won by the use of X.

The assumption of analysis of covariance is that the effect of X is completely resolvable into the regression line. Thus, if the group treatments are to have any effect at all upon the ultimate Y-score, then the locus of the effect must be in that which is residual after the effect of the regression line is removed. This is exactly what is achieved by the formula. It subtracts from the variation in Y the amount of variation which is contained in the regression line.

In effect what is achieved in this subtraction is the scoring of each individual in accordance with his place on the regression line as determined by his X-score. Thus, in effect, each subject is scored in terms of the deviation from the place where his initial level would put him.

We might point out, in this connection, an advantage of this method over the use of difference scores. In difference score analysis the subject is graded from a base of initial performance. In the analysis of covariance the subject is graded *from a base of his expected score* which is determined by the experience which we acquire in the experiment itself, namely, the degree of association between Y and X.

In applying the formula, we do it twice: once on the total, which is a compounding of both Within and Between Group effects, and once on the Within Group effect. In the one case we remove the Total regression and in the other we remove the Within Group regression.

Thus, the remaining variation which exists among the groups is the variation among the means after the removal of these effects. Each time that the formula is applied a degree of freedom associated with the regression is lost. The application of the formula twice does not change the number of degrees of freedom associated with the Between Groups, since the difference between the reduced degrees of freedom remains the same.

Thus the test of the resulting Between Groups and Within Groups is exactly a test of the remaining variation after the regression is removed, and provides us with information on the training methods in which the initial variation among the groups has no role.

THE ADJUSTED MEANS

The knowledge that our groups differ significantly is, however, not enough. The original Y-means are now no longer adequate for our purposes. It can occur, for example, that one group may be superior on the initial Y-mean, but be inferior after we have made the adjustment for the X-scores. It is incumbent upon us to recompute the means, based on the nature of the regression. It is only in this way that we can say that one method of training is better than another method of training.

The critical regression is that of the Within Groups. It has removed from it all effects of association between X- and Y-means. This is the regression which we use in attempting to determine what the corrected Y-means are.

By dividing the SSxy by the SSx, Within Groups, we get exactly the slope of the regression line. For each group we determine the X-mean. On the basis of the X-mean and the regression line we determine the expected mean for each group. This result is then exactly what we would expect from each group on the basis of the X-means only. In terms of our assumption, then, the way in which the actual obtained Y-mean deviates from the expected place on the regression line must be due to the effect of other things than the X-scores, group effects and random effects. Thus, the deviation of the Y-mean from the regression line should be taken as its corrected value, and the test of the significance of the variation among these is exactly a test of the significance of the variation with the effects of X removed. This latter test is the test which we discussed previously.

THE PROBLEM OF HOMOGENEITY OF CORRELATION

In the determination of the Within Groups regression, what is done, in effect, is the equating of all groups with respect to their means (by considering only deviations from their group means). One might think of this as the movement of all of the groups in a scatterplot, maintaining their internal relations, but making all of the means coincide.

This, however, entails the assumption of homogeneity of the regressions, that they only differ from one another insofar as they might be expected to differ due to random variation. Technically, the assumption of homogeneity is made in the procedures which have been discussed already.

In addition to the technical considerations—for statistical technical considerations are only *sometimes* important in practical research—the matter of homogeneity is extremely important in the kind of research to which we are directing our attention.

If the groups are not homogeneous with respect to regression, it means that the different training methods are related differently to the initial scores in a way which is quite different from that revealed by the study of the Y-means. *If we were to find that there is heterogeneity of the regression it would mean that the different training methods exploit the initial level of the subjects differently.* In effect it would mean that there is an interaction between the training method and the initial level. The quest for a decision among training methods in which we attempt to equate subjects for their initial level becomes then relatively pointless in comparison with this other finding, in addition to making this other analysis technically untenable.

The test for the homogeneity of regression is easily effected by procedures closely related to the ones which we have already discussed. By completely analogous methods we compute for each group the SS dev. from reg., where the regression line is that for the individual group itself. These are then summed, as are the corresponding degrees of freedom, again losing a degree of freedom for each regression line.

Obviously, if the result of this computation is substantially smaller than our previous SS dev. from regression, then the only explanation can be that the individual regression lines fit their data better than the average one we have considered, and hence, there must be substantial variation among the regression lines. If in applying the F-test to the difference between these values, we find that it is significant, we must conclude that there is heterogeneity among the regression lines.

Now, if this should be the case, it will be found within the data themselves, and does not require that new data be collected. And even if the initial quest is frustrated, such a finding has considerable value in itself with respect to elucidating the effect of the training methods. It would show that some methods may be better for some people and other training methods would be better for other people. The major implication for training would be not the simple decision that one method is better than another, but rather that there must be a closer matching of training with the characteristics that the individual brings to the training situation.

Fortunately, however, we have enough accumulated wisdom and experience in connection with the interaction of initial level of the subject and the effect of training. Crudely stated, we do not attempt to teach higher mathematics to people who have only a knowledge of very elementary mathematics. The correlations between X and Y for such a group would at best be negligible. If we were interested in teaching higher mathematics to a group, it would only be to a group for whom we might suspect some substantial correlation between X and Y.

Obviously, if we had both groups, we would find that the assumption of homogeneity of regression would fail, and would certainly show up quite quickly the triviality of such an experiment. In brief, then, if we are at least minimally intelligent about the choice of the subjects whom we use in such experimentation, with a view to analyzing the results by the methods of analysis of covariance, it is generally likely that the assumption will be satisfied.

The problem which we have posed of the interaction of subject level with training method is one which calls for other methods of analysis and other considerations.

The Matched Group Design
in Educational Research

George Douglas Mayo and Alexander A. Longo

*Naval Air Station, Millington, Tennessee
and U.S. Military Academy*

[This paper is concerned with the third of the three research methods mentioned in the introduction to Part III. In common with the other two, it was developed for use in ongoing educational situations where it has been utilized successfully. The methods described by DuBois and by Bakan, however, depend upon statistical controls, while the method described by Mayo and Longo depends upon what might be referred to as quasi-experimental control. The procedure seeks to avoid several of the problems that have tended to cause many educational researchers to feel that the use of matched groups is poor research strategy.

Doubtless, the basic method described in this paper has been used many times before. The paper is thought, however, to make explicit the practical problems involved in the use of matched groups in educational research to a somewhat greater extent than before and to describe a partial solution.]

The matched group design in educational and psychological research has a strong technical, as well as logical, appeal. The advantage of using the correlation term in comparison of treatment groups is well known. However, practical problems associated with the matched group design in ongoing educational and training situations have restricted its use.

Some of the problems associated with the use of this design, as ordinarily employed in applied research, are reviewed below. It is usually considered necessary to identify and use a matching variable which correlates satisfactorily with the criterion measure, prior to differential treatment of the groups. This may require preliminary study in order to identify an appropriate matching variable. If the experimenter matches his subjects on a variable that later turns out to correlate zero with the criterion, no statistical or logical advantage accrues from the matching process.

In large training operations, such as those of military and industrial organizations, often the same course convenes on a weekly, biweekly, or monthly basis. As a rule, subjects beginning the course on successive convening dates must be combined in order to arrive at an N of the desired size. This requires matching within each convening class, and also requires as many sections as there are treatments to be compared. Further, within the relatively small number of subjects convening on a given date, satisfactory matching may be difficult and may require eliminating subjects from the sample whose scores do not match those of other subjects.

One of the more serious limitations associated with the conventional matched group design stems from the loss of subjects during the experiment for reasons that are uncorrelated with the measures used in the study. These losses include absence from one or more treatment sessions due to illness, emergencies of various types, and disciplinary or other administrative matters. As a rule perfectly matched groups do not remain perfectly matched over any substantial time span under real life conditions. The usual expedient when something happens to one member of a pair is to eliminate the other member of the pair also, if the matching procedure utilized the pairing process. If the original matching involved only equal means and standard deviations, scores from one group or from all groups are sometimes eliminated in an effort to match the groups completing the various treatments, on the basis of the matching variable. This procedure is seldom completely satisfactory. This is especially true if more than two groups are involved. A third possibility is to assume that any losses from the groups are on a random basis and therefore no adjustment should be made. Despite the above partial solutions, most researchers would prefer not to have to cope with the problem of losing subjects from matched groups.

THE PROCEDURE

In recent months the writers have been developing, and experimenting with a matching procedure which seems to have most of the advantages of conventional matching; or pairing of subjects, but is not as subject to the limitations of conventional matching mentioned above. Basically, the procedure involves pairing of subjects from two or more treatment pools after the completion of training or other treatment, but without knowledge of the performance of the subjects, or any other information concerning the subjects, except the score made on the matching variable.

In implementing the procedure subjects are assigned to treatment pools in an essentially unselected manner, with a view to avoiding any major systematic differences between the treatment pools from which the subjects later will be matched. Upon completion of the training, or other treatment, subjects are paired or matched on the basis of a score obtained prior to the beginning of the experiment. This matching is accomplished manually from the treatment pools of subjects, each individual in the pool being represented by a card which contains only his name and score on the matching variable. This step may be accomplished by data processing equipment, if desired. Any members of the treatment pools who did not receive the standard treatment accorded their group because of illness, administrative matters, or for other reasons uncorrelated with the criterion measure, are eliminated from the pools prior to the matching process.

It should be noted that the procedure does not require irrevocable identification of the matching variable prior to completion of the training, or other treatment. Two or more tests may be given prior to the beginning of training and their correlation with the criterion variable determined after the training is completed. The test having the best correlation with the criterion measure may then be selected as a basis for matching the subjects from the treatment pools. If the use of more than two or three prospective predictors is used there may be some difficulty due to capitalizing upon chance factors, which may result in a somewhat higher correlation term than is warranted, but with no more than three or four prospective matching variables this should not introduce a very large error.

If the control group pool contains a substantially larger number than the experimental group pool, pairing of individuals with identical scores is facilitated. It is not unusual in ongoing training situations for the control group to be large enough to permit identical matching of virtually all members of the experimental group with a member from the control group pool. Identical matching of individuals from one or more treatment pools also is facilitated by virtue of the fact that personnel entering training on different convening dates may be grouped into a large pool for each treatment, which facilitates matching. As previously noted, under the conventional matching procedure, matching must be accomplished separately for each convening class.

When the control group pool contains subjects having a certain score on the matching variable, in excess of the number required to match the subjects having this score in the experimental treatment pools, the decision as to which subjects should be selected from the control group pool is made by use of a table of random numbers.

Any effects of regression resulting from matching subjects from pools that differ widely are not corrected or otherwise affected by the procedure described herein. These effects were described by Rulon (1941) and Thorndike (1942). More recently they have been reviewed by Campbell and Stanley (1963). When matching is accomplished from pools that are quite comparable, however, regression effects should not pose a serious problem.

EXAMPLES OF IMPLEMENTATION

The matching procedure described above has been tried empirically in three studies conducted in an ongoing training situation, to determine whether or not practical problems not foreseen at the time the procedure was conceived would develop. A brief description of these three studies, primarily from the standpoint of matching, follows.

The first study (Longo and Mayo, 1965) compared the performance of a group of 200 students in a basic electronics course who were taught by means of programmed instruction with a control group of 200 students who received their instruction by means of conventional classroom instruction. Table 10 shows the basic information pertaining to this study. The two treatment pools each contained 206 students. Almost perfect pairing of 200 subjects from the two groups was accomplished, resulting in identical means and standard deviations on the matching variable. The matching variable was the grade made in a short course in Aviation Familiarization which preceded the training

Table 10

MEANS AND STANDARD DEVIATIONS FOR
CONVENTIONAL AND PROGRAMMED INSTRUCTION GROUPS
(N = 200 in each group)

Test	Means		t	Standard Deviations		t
	Conv. Group	Prog. Group		Conv. Group	Prog. Group	
Matching Var.	79.61	79.61		7.29	7.29	
Prog. Inst.	37.22	38.50	1.95*	7.55	7.05	1.01
Conv. Inst.	40.40	39.32	1.87	6.48	6.40	.17

*t value of 1.97 required for significance at .05 level.

Table 11

MEANS AND STANDARD DEVIATIONS FOR REGULAR AND
EXPERIMENTAL ELECTRONICS FUNDAMENTALS GROUPS
(N = 154 in each group)

| Test | Means | | t | Standard Deviations | | t |
	Reg. Group	Exp. Group		Reg. Group	Exp. Group	
Matching Var.	80.21	80.21		7.30	7.30	
Criterion Var.	76.18	70.88	5.21*	10.17	10.14	.04

*t value of 2.61 required for .01 significance level.

in basic electronics. The correlation between the matching variable
and the two criterion variables was approximately .45.

The second study (Longo and Mayo, 1966a) compared the achievement of 154 students who received an original course in electronics
fundamentals with 154 students who received a revised course covering
the same material. The revised course was 14 weeks in length while the
original course was five weeks longer. Each of the 154 members in the
experimental group pool was paired with one of the 637 members of
the control group pool having an identical score. The matching variable
was the same as that used in the first study, mentioned above. In this
instance the correlation of the matching variable with the achievement
test given at the end of the course was .38. The basic information pertaining to this study is shown in Table 11.

The third study (Longo and Mayo, 1966b) was conducted in a school
which trains technicians who maintain and repair airborne radar equipment. This study involved the matching of four treatment groups. The
groups were matched from pools of subjects receiving instruction in
courses that were 30 weeks, 27 weeks, 25 weeks, or 22 weeks in length.
These data are shown in Table 12. Each of the matched groups con-

Table 12

MEANS AND STANDARD DEVIATIONS FOR FOUR GROUPS
RECEIVING COURSES OF DIFFERENT LENGTH PREPARATORY
TO EMPLOYMENT AS AIRBORNE RADAR TECHNICIANS
(N = 27 in each group)

| Training Received | Matching Variable | | Criterion Variable | |
	Mean	S.D.	Mean*	S.D.
30 weeks	82.89	5.13	55.56	4.34
27 weeks	82.89	5.13	53.78	6.82
25 weeks	82.89	5.13	51.70	5.49
22 weeks	82.89	5.13	50.30	4.21

*F = 6.04.   F value of 4.08 required for .01 significance level.

tained 27 subjects with identical scores. The matching variable was the same as in the other two studies. The average correlation between the matching variable and the achievement measure in the four treatment groups in this instance was .29.

The empirical tryout of the procedure involving matching from treatment pools after the application of different treatments, suggests that few, if any, practical problems tend to be associated with the use of the procedure when only two groups are involved. This is especially true when one of the treatment pools (usually the control group pool) is larger than the experimental pool. Matching becomes more difficult when more than two treatment pools are involved, but was considered fairly satisfactory in the study involving four treatments. The four treatment pools contained 77, 56, 46, and 62 subjects, respectively. Therefore the maximum possible number of matched subjects was 46. It turned out that 27 subjects from each of the four groups had identical scores on the matching variable. The remaining subjects were not included in the analysis. This application of the procedure was less satisfactory than in the case of the other two and suggests that other experimental designs may be preferable when more than two treatment groups are involved.

SUMMARY

Despite its strong logical and technical appeal, the employment of the matched group design in applied psychological research has been restricted by practical problems associated with its use. A procedure which circumvents several of the problems of conventional matching can be described. Basically, the procedure involves pairing of subjects from two or more treatment pools after the completion of training or other treatment, but without knowledge of the performance of the subjects. Three empirical tryouts of the procedure were summarized. The procedure worked quite well when only two groups were involved and was fairly satisfactory when applied to four groups. Other experimental designs may be better when more than two groups are involved. It was concluded that matching from treatment pools after differential treatment of the pools warrants more extensive use in applied educational and psychological research than it has been accorded in the past.

Some Nonintellectual Predictors
of Classroom Success

Carl J. Spies

Kent State University

[The first three papers in Part III were concerned primarily with research methods in an educational research environment. The final three papers are examples of research using one of the methods described, correlational analysis, and showing the results achieved. Spies' paper is concerned primarily with noncognitive predictors of two criteria in classroom work, residual gain and achievement as usually measured in the classroom. Inclusion of these two criteria in the same study provides information as to how readily the two are predictable from certain noncognitive tests. In addition to the noncognitive predictors three aptitude tests also are included in the study.]

The purpose of this study, made at Naval Air Station, Millington, was to discover nonintellectual predictors of that part of several achievement criteria which was not predictable from aptitude measures. The criterion of principal interest was residual gain in learning, defined as that part of final status which is uncorrelated with initial status. The predictability of final status from nonintellectual predictors was also of interest.

The nonintellectual predictors under investigation included personality needs as measured by the Edwards Personal Preference Schedule, personality traits as measured by the Guilford-Zimmerman Temperament Survey, interest as measured by the Navy Vocational Interest Inventory, speed of learning as measured by the DuBois-Bunch Speed of Learning Test, and persistence as measured by a modification of a test suggested by Glickman.

The subjects were naval trainees in a 19-week electronics fundamentals course. The course was divided into Phase A of four weeks, Phase 1 of seven weeks and Phases 2 and 3 of four weeks each. The eight weeks of Phases 2 and 3 was the part of the course selected for investigation. As a measure of initial status for men beginning Phase 2, the score on the final examination in Phase 1 was used. Phase 1 was concerned primarily with basic electronics, while Phases 2 and 3 were concerned with the use of electronic components in more complicated systems. Thus it was felt that knowledge of components acquired in Phase 1 would constitute a good measure of the knowledge to be brought by the trainee to his study of more involved systems.

The battery of nonintellectual tests was administered during the first week of Phase A. Scores on the Navy General Classification Test and Arithmetic Test were available for all trainees.

The sample was drawn from six successive classes in the Electronics Fundamentals School. The few women and marines were eliminated from the analysis. Also, there was an attrition of from 10 per cent to 15 per cent in the classes tested. Finally, a few men were excluded from the analysis for failure to properly complete all of the tests. The final total in the analysis was 418.

The measure of final status was that part of the final examination in the course which dealt with the material covered in Phases 2 and 3. The residual gain criterion was that part of this measure of final status which was uncorrelated with initial status. The correlation between initial and final status was .65. This considerably reduced the reliability of the residual variance to be predicted. Of all the predictors used (32 in all) only GCT, ARI, n-Ach from the EPPS and electronics interest from the Navy Vocational Interest Inventory were significantly correlated with final status at the .01 level. All of these except n-Ach were also significantly correlated with initial status. Thus, when the residual gain criterion was used, the predictors had lost some of their effectiveness. A summary of the correlations between the predictors and the two criteria, residual gain and final status, is presented in Table 13.

It can be seen that residual gain is correlated with aptitude measures .29 and that n-Ach as an additional predictor increases the multiple to .33. Interest does not contribute significantly to this multiple correlation. In prediction of final status the aptitude measures and both of the nonintellectual predictors contribute uniquely to the multiple correlation. In all cases, predictors correlate more highly with final status than

Table 13

CORRELATIONS OF PREDICTORS WITH RESIDUAL GAIN AND FINAL STATUS

Predictors	Correlation with Residual Gain	Correlation with Final Status
1	.19**	.32**
2	.27**	.34**
3	.17**	.23**
4	.11*	.22**
1 + 2	.29**	.42**
1 + 2 + 3	.33**	.46**
1 + 2 + 3 + 4	.34**	.49**
3 + 4	.20**	.30**
(3.124)	.14**	.18**
(4.123)	.08	.18**
(3.12)	.15**	.18**
(4.12)	.09	.18**

N = 418

1 = GCT
2 = ARITH
3 = n-Ach
4 = Electronics Interest

* Significant at .05 level
** Significant at .01 level

with residual gain, but the correlations with residual gain are fairly substantial.

As a followup the grades in basic, or Class A, school were obtained for as many of the subjects in this study as possible. The A-schools follow the fundamentals schools. It was impossible to obtain information on all of the subjects because some did not go directly to an A-school and some of the A-schools had so few men that it was not worthwhile to make an analysis. With final grade in A-school as a measure of final status, two sets of residuals were obtained: (a) those with the original measure of initial status used as initial status, (b) those with the final grade in fundamentals school as a measure of initial school status.

Only electronics interest was significantly related to the residual gain between end of fundamentals school and end of A-school in one of the two schools analyzed. For the longer period using Phase 1 grade as the initial measure, the electronics interest measure was a significant predictor in both of the A-schools analyzed (N = 102 and N = 162). In one of the A-schools GCT was also significantly correlated with residual gain and added significantly to the multiple (.25** to .35**). In neither case was n-Ach significantly correlated with residual gain. It seems strange that n-Ach should be correlated only with residual gain from end of Phase 1 to the end of the fundamentals course, but not with residual gain from end of Phase 1 to end of the A-school course. It is interesting to note the increase in predictive power of interest over the longer period of instruction.

To summarize, it has been shown that residual gain as well as final status is a predictable criterion of learning, that several nonintellectual predictors are significantly correlated with both residual gain and final status, and that a small but significant addition to a multiple correlation between aptitude measures and either of these criteria can be made by use of at least one nonintellectual predictor.

Programmed Instruction
and the Ability to Learn

James L. Wardrop

University of Illinois

[Continuing with application of correlational methodology to educational research, Wardrop's paper applies these procedures to the problem of predicting school performance from a miniature educational situation. It is well known that performance in one training course often is an excellent predictor of performance in a similar, more extensive course. Wardrop uses a programmed instruction booklet and two other miniature learning situations. He succeeds in demonstrating both the value of the correlational method and of programmed instruction as a miniature learning situation.]

This study was carried out in order to investigate the use of programmed instruction as a miniature learning situation for predicting performance in a subsequent large-scale (classroom) learning situation.

There are five assumptions or findings on which this study is based.

First, intelligence and the ability to learn are apparently not entirely the same. As early as 1901, Wissler found little or no relationship between scholastic achievement and a number of mental tests developed by Cattell. In more recent years, studies by Woodrow (1938, 1946) and Simrall (1947) indicate that intelligence and learning are not the same, and that the factors or abilities measured by intelligence tests are only partially those involved in the learning process. In view of the findings such as these, it should be possible to improve upon the use of intelligence tests for selection and prediction—particularly in educational situations (Sorensen, 1963).

Secondly, the ability to learn seems not to be a unitary function. The findings of Wimms (1907), in one of the earliest studies in this area, set the pattern. He found no correlation between gain in two similar learning tasks. The majority of subsequent studies in this area report a similar lack of general learning ability (Allison, 1960; Atkinson, 1929; Hall, 1936; Husband, 1939; Stake, 1961).

In the third place, a potentially valuable approach to the prediction of learning is through the use of learning tests, or miniature learning situations. Such an approach, suggested by Frederiksen et al. (1947), has been used in a number of investigations of learning and human ability (see Allison, 1954; 1956; and 1960).

Fourth, a major problem in the investigation of learning has been the statistic of measurement of learning. Most studies in the literature make use of one of three different measures: measures based on a single evaluation of proficiency at the conclusion of practice or training; crude gain, the difference between measures of final and initial proficiency; and per cent gain, usually defined as the ratio of crude gain to initial status. Two other measures of learning have appeared in the literature in recent years: parameters of individual learning curves, involving curve-fitting and the determination of certain parameters of the curves so obtained; and residual gain, defined as that portion of the measure of final performance which is statistically independent of initial status. Because it offers the advantages of consistency, adaptability, and statistical logic, residual gain is the measure employed in this study.

Finally, programmed instruction provides a controlled, organized miniature learning situation amenable to careful, periodic assessment of the progress of learning, particularly initial and final proficiency. According to Green (1962, p. 112), the "learning process as it is controlled by programmed instruction differs in no essential way from the learning process as it is controlled in the classroom." The particular idea of using teaching machine performance to develop a measure of learning ability has been proposed by Sorenson (1963).

METHOD

Subjects.   The subjects used in this study were trainees at the Naval Air Station, Millington, Tenn. Two groups were used: 148 Students in the Aviation Mechanical Fundamentals School [AMFU(A)], and 330 in the Aviation Electronics Fundamentals School [AFU(A)]. The two groups were tested together in groups of about 45 over a period of eleven weeks, before they began school. Average age of the subjects was 19 years, and the average educational level was 12 years. The AFU(A) students averaged about one standard deviation above the means on subtests of the Navy Basic Test Battery, a test of general intelligence, while students in AMFU(A) school averaged only one or two points above the means on this battery.

Tests and Procedure. The General Classification subtest of the Basic Test Battery, a group test of verbal intelligence, was used as the measure of intelligence. The learning tests used were the DuBois-Bunch Learning Test, a simple perceptual learning task adapted for group administration (DuBois and Bunch, 1949); and a Numbers Test, in which subjects were to trace, in sequence, numbers from 1 through 60 printed in apparently random positions on a page. (A fuller description of this test can be found in Hackett, 1964.) Each of these tests consisted of ten trials, from which an initial score (average score on the first two trials) and a final score (average score on the two final trials) were obtained.

The programmed instruction learning measure was obtained from performance on a linear program on study skills. Before this 214-frame program, subjects were given a 27-item pretest over the material in the program; after completing the program, they were given an equivalent 27-item posttest over the same material. Included in the program were a number of test items, frames in which no answers were supplied and the students were required to write their responses.

The other test given during this preschool session was a pretest over the material taught in the two fundamentals schools. The items on this pretest were taken from a pool of items used in the preparation of examinations in the schools. This test was used as a measure of initial knowledge or proficiency.

Measures of final status were not the same for the two schools. For AFU(A) students, the final average in the first (five-week) phase of the 19-week school was used, while the school final average was used for the AMFU(A) students, since this is only a five-week course.

Testing sessions were held once weekly, and each lasted approximately three hours. The learning tests, the How-to-Study program, and the school pretest were given in this session.

In the data analysis, a matrix of intercorrelations of all variables in the study was obtained for each school. From these matrices, the correlations of the residual gain measures with all other variables were found. Finally, intercorrelations among these residuals were obtained. The residuals used were gain (learning) on the DuBois-Bunch Learning Test, learning on the Numbers Test, learning by means of programmed instruction, and learning in the classroom.

RESULTS

Table 14 shows the correlations of the predictors with two criteria, phase (or school) final average and a gain measure of classroom learning. In AFU(A) school, the programmed instruction learning measure correlated .27 with the gain measure of classroom learning. This was significantly greater than the correlations of the other learning measures with this criterion. The intelligence measure (GCT) correlated .28 with the gain measure of classroom learning. In AMFU(A) school, the programmed instruction learning measure correlated .23 with the gain measure of classroom learning. Again, this correlation was significantly greater than those involving the other learning tests. The intelligence measure (GCT) correlated .28 with the gain measure in this school.

Table 14
PREDICTOR-CRITERION CORRELATIONS

| | Criterion | |
Predictor	AFU(A) School	AMFU(A) School
GCT	.28	.30
Gain on DuBois-Bunch Test	.08	.13
Gain on Numbers Test	−.02	.01
Gain on Programmed Instruction	.27	.23

DISCUSSION

The results indicate that programmed instruction performance is more closely related to classroom performance than is performance on the other learning tests employed. (It should be noted that neither of the other tests is a verbal learning test; rather, both are tests involving perceptual-motor skills.) In addition, when considered in combination with the intelligence measure, the programmed instruction learning measure raises the correlation with classroom performance (final average) from .30 to .33 in AMFU(A) school and from .28 to .37 in AFU(A) school.

The results tend to support the view that properly conceived and constructed learning tests can be successfully used to provide predictions of subsequent classroom learning. The clear superiority of the programmed instruction learning task provides a basis for speculation about other kinds of miniature learning situations which might prove to be effective sources of valid predictions of subsequent performance.

Further studies in this area would have not only the practical value of determining the most valid predictors of classroom performance, but could also provide data concerning the unity or diversity of human learning abilities.

The Relationship Between
Learning and Intelligence[1]

Ronald P. Carver

American Institutes for Research

[The final example of an application of correlational analysis to
educational research is an investigation by Carver in which he
takes a new look at a very old question, the relationship of intelligence to learning. It is always possible that the inability
of researchers to find support for the early definition of intelligence, as ability to learn, was a function of the methods and measures used in their investigations. Carver reasons that if we now
have somewhat better methods and measures, it might be worthwhile to apply them to this question. His application makes interesting reading both from the standpoint of method and of results.]

In a study of relationship between learning and intelligence, 269 U. S.
Navy enlisted men were given a battery of seven learning tests. The
service men were students awaiting entry into one of the technical
schools at the Navy Air Technical Training Center at Millington,
Tennessee. The nature of the learning tests was somewhat varied. Two
of the seven tests involved initial and final measures on programmed
instructional materials. These are Tests 1 and 2 in Table 15.

The Electronics Programmed Instruction was a linear programmed
booklet on Ohm's Law and Powers of Ten. The material for Test 2 was

---

[1] A subsequent version of this paper was published in the *Journal of Educational
Measurement*, 1967, 4, 133-136.

Table 15

INTERCORRELATIONS OF SEVEN LEARNING VARIABLES* AND INTELLIGENCE (above diagonal); RESIDUAL CORRELATION MATRIX AFTER EXTRACTION OF THREE FACTORS (below diagonal); ROTATED FACTOR LOADINGS AND COMMUNALITIES (extreme right); AND CORRELATIONS OF LEARNING VARIABLES WITH INTELLIGENCE AFTER CORRECTION FOR ATTENUATION OF LEARNING VARIABLES (bottom of table)

| | 1 | 2 | 3 | 4 | 5 | 6 | 7 | 8 | Rotated Factor Loadings | | | h^2 |
									I	II	III	
LEARNING TASKS												
1. Electronics Programmed Instruction		.37	.23	.14	.04	.18	.06	.26	.48	.21	.02	.27
2. Behavior Programmed Instruction	.02		.24	.19	.14	.13	.07	.44	.66	.14	.14	.48
3. Nonsense Syllable Learning Test	-.01	-.03		.22	.04	.09	.16	.19	.33	.39	-.03	.26
4. Color Code Learning Test	-.02	.01	.03		.14	.12	.16	.12	.18	.34	.14	.17
5. DuBois-Bunch Learning Test	-.02	.01	.00	.02		.19	.14	.16	.06	.09	.51	.27
6. Alternate Form, DuBois-Bunch	.06	-.04	-.03	-.02	.00		.18	.17	.14	.19	.34	.17
7. Numbers Tracing Test	.01	.02	.00	-.02	-.01	.02		-.04	-.07	.48	.22	.29
INTELLIGENCE												
8. General Classification Test	-.03	.00	.03	-.01	.00	.00	-.01		.62	-.08	.25	.46
(General Classification Test correlations corrected for attenuation of the gain scores)	.31	.51	.22	.13	.23	.22	-.05					

N = 269. Significance Levels: .05, r = .12; .01, r = .16; .001, r = .20.
*Learning variables all in terms of residual gain.

the first two sets of Holland and Skinner's (1961) programmed textbook "Analysis of Behavior." Test 3 was a group Nonsense Syllable Learning Test. Test 4, Color Code Learning Test; Test 5, DuBois-Bunch Learning Test, and Test 6, an alternate form of the DuBois-Bunch, were all essentially perceptual learning tasks while Test 7, labeled Tracing Numbers Test, involved visual scanning and motor tracing.

The measure of intelligence was the General Classification Test. This test measures verbal ability by testing comprehension of word meaning and verbal relationships. It is a part of the Basic Test Battery given to all Naval enlisted personnel.

Scores on the learning tests were residual gain measures, residual gain defined as that portion of final status which is uncorrelated with initial status. Stated differently, residual gain is final score less the portion predictable from initial score.

In the table all but one of the correlations of the gain scores with intelligence were significant at the .05 level. The only insignificant correlation was with the Numbers Tracing Test, a task which is logically unrelated to verbal intelligence.

A principle axis factor analysis was made of the intercorrelations of the gain variables and intelligence. The communalities were estimated by iteration. Three factors were extracted and rotated to a varimax criterion.

The highest loadings on Factor I were with those variables which have high verbal content. The two programmed instructional tasks, with loadings of .48 and .66 respectively, were of a verbal nature as well as the Nonsense Syllable Learning Test which had a loading of .33. The verbal intelligence measure had its highest loading on this factor, .62. In contrast, the task which involved visual scanning and motor tracing, the Number Tracing Test had a negative factor loading of −.07. These loadings prompted a verbal label for Factor I. Factors II and III seem to be almost unique to the learning tasks as their loadings on intelligence were only −.08 and .25. Factor III has its highest loadings on the DuBois-Bunch Learning Test and its Alternate Form, while Factor II in general has its lowest loadings on these two variables. No labels were attached to these two factors.

It was reasoned that if intelligence and learning were not related then there should be one factor which had its only predominant loading on intelligence and another factor which had its high loadings on the learning variables and low or zero loadings on the intelligence variable. This prediction was not supported by the evidence. On the contrary, evidence was found for a verbal factor on which both the verbal learning tasks and intelligence were highly weighted and two additional factors which were largely specific to the learning tasks.

In conclusion, the results were interpreted as negating the generalization that learning and intelligence are unrelated when a gain measure of learning is used. The evidence used for this negation was twofold: (1) the significant correlations between intelligence and the gain scores on the learning tasks demonstrate a relationship; and (2) the factor loadings on Factor I, the verbal factor, demonstrate that one of the major factors which underlies verbal intelligence is also the major factor underlying the learning variables of a verbal nature.

Although these data were interpreted as negating the broad generalization that intelligence is unrelated to learning two things should be pointed out: (1) the relationship found was significant but low, and (2) two factors were found which were largely specific to learning tasks.

REFERENCES

Allison, R. B. Learning measures as predictors of success in Torpedoman's Mates School. Office of Naval Research Technical Report. Princeton, N. J.: *Educational Testing Service*, 1954.

Allison, R. B. Learning measures as predictors of success in Pipefitter and Metalsmith Schools. Office of Naval Research Technical Report. Princeton, N. J.: *Educational Testing Service*, 1956.

Allison, R. B. Learning parameters and human abilities. Office of Naval Research Technical Report. Princeton, N. J.: *Educational Testing Service*, 1960.

Anderson, J. E. The limitations of infant and preschool tests in the measurement of intelligence. *Journal of Psychology*, 1939, 8, 351-379.

Atkinson, W. R. The relation of intelligence and of mechanical speeds to the various stages of learning. *Journal of Experimental Psychology*, 1929, 12, 89-112.

Bakan, D. The test of significance in psychological research. *Psychological Bulletin*, 1966, 6, 423-437.

Block, Virginia. Reading progress of fourth grade pupils and implications for school practice. Unpublished Ed. D. dissertation. Stanford University, 1950.

Bridgman, P. W. *The logic of modern physics.* New York: Macmillan, 1927.

Bush, R. R. and Mosteller, F. *Stochastic models for learning.* New York: Wiley, 1955.

Campbell, D. T. Operational delineation of "what is learned" via the transposition experiment. *Psychological Review*, 1954, 61, 167-174.

Campbell, D. T. and Fiske, D. W. Convergent and discriminant validation by the multitrait-multimethod matrix. *Psychological Bulletin*, 1959, 56, 81-105.

Campbell, D. T. and Stanley, J. C. Experimental and quasi-experimental designs for research on teaching. In N. L. Gage (Ed.), *Handbook of research on teaching: A project of the American Educational Research Association.* Chicago: Rand McNally, 1963.

Cattell, R. B. *Factor analysis.* New York: Harper, 1952.

Chapman, J. Crosby. The learning curve in typewriting. *Journal of Applied Psychology*, 1919, 3, 252-268.

Coombs, C. *A theory of data.* New York: Wiley, 1963.

Cronbach, L. J. The two disciplines of scientific psychology. *The American Psychologist*, 1957, 12, 671-684.

DuBois, P. H. *Multivariate correlational analysis.* New York: Harper, 1957.

DuBois, P. H. An analysis of Guttman's simplex. *Psychometrika*, 1960, 25, 173-182.

DuBois, P. H. and Bunch, M. E. A new technique for studying group-learning. *American Journal of Psychology*, 1949, 62, 272-278.

Estes, W. K. Toward a statistical theory of learning. *Psychological Review*, 1950, 57, 94-107.

Ferguson, G. A. On learning and human ability. *Canadian Journal of Psychology*, 1954, 8, 95-112.

Ferguson, G. A. Transfer and human ability. *Canadian Journal of Psychology*, 1956, 10, 121-131.

Fleishman, E. A. A comparative study of aptitude patterns in unskilled and skilled psychomotor performances. *Journal of Applied Psychology*, 1957, 41, 263-272.

Fleishman, E. A. and Hempel, W. E., Jr. Changes in factor structure of a complex psychomotor test as a function of practice. *Psychometrika*, 1954, 19, 239-252.

Fleishman, E. A. and Hempel, W. E., Jr. The relation between abilities and improvement with practice in a visual discrimination reaction task. *Journal of Experimental Psychology*, 1955, 49, 301-312.

Frankmann, Judith P. Effect of amount of interpolated learning and time interval before test on retention in rats. *Journal of Experimental Psychology*, 1957, 54, 462-466.

Franzen, R. A comment on partial correlation. *Journal of Educational Psychology*, 1928, 19, 194-197.

Frederiksen, N., Carstater, E. D., and Stuit, D. B. Problems for further study. In D. B. Stuit (Ed.), *Personnel research and test development in the Bureau of Naval Personnel*. Princeton, N. J.: Princeton University Press, 1947.

Gagné, R. M. Military training and principles of learning. *American Psychologist*, 1962, 17, 83-91.

Gagné, R. M. Curriculum research and the promotion of learning. In R. W. Tyler, R. M. Gagné and Michael Scriven *Perspectives of Curriculum Evaluation*, AERA Monograph 1. Chicago: Rand McNally, 1967.

Green, E. J. *The learning process and programmed instruction*. New York: Holt, Rinehart, and Winston, 1962.

Guilford, J. P. The structure of intellect. *Psychological Bulletin*, 1956, 53, 267-293.

Gulliksen, H. *Theory of mental tests*. New York: Wiley, 1950.

Gulliksen, H. Mathematical solutions for psychological problems. Technical Report on ONR Research Contract Nonr 1858(15) and NSF Grant G-642, Princeton University and Educational Testing Service, 1958, 1-54.

Guttman, L. A new approach to factor analysis: the Radex. In P. F. Lazarsfeld, *Mathematical thinking in the social sciences*. Glencoe, Illinois: The Free Press, 1954.

Guttman, L. Empirical verification of the Radex structure of mental abilities and personality traits. *Educational and Psychological Measurement*, 1957, 17, 391-407.

Hackett, E. V. The use of learning tests in the analysis of training. In P. H. DuBois and K. M. Wientge (Eds.), *Strategies of research on learning in educational settings*. St. Louis: Washington University, 1964.

Hall, C. S. Intercorrelations of measures of human learning. *Psychological Review*, 1936, 43, 179-195.

Harlow, H. F. The formation of learning sets. *Psychological Review*, 1949, 56, 51-65.

Hebb, D. O. *The organization of behavior; a neurological theory*. New York: Wiley, 1949.

Holland, James G. and Skinner, B. F. *Analysis of behavior*. New York: McGraw-Hill, 1961.

Hollingworth, H. L. Influence of caffeine on the speed and quality of performance in typewriting. *Psychological Review*, 1912, 19, 66-73.

Hull, C. L. *Essentials of behavior*. New Haven: Yale University Press, 1951.

Husband, R. W. Intercorrelations among learning abilities: I. *Journal of Genetic Psychology*, 1939, 55, 353-364.

Longo, A. A. and Mayo, G. D. Comparison of conventional and programmed instruction in teaching avionics fundamentals. Technical Bulletin STB-66-16, U. S. Naval Personnel Research Activity, San Diego, California, 1965.

Longo, A. A. and Mayo, G. D. An experiment in basic airborne electronics training, part 1, effect of reduction in training time upon knowledge of electronics fundamentals. Technical Bulletin STB 67-8, U. S. Naval Personnel Research Activity, San Diego, California, 1966.

Longo, A. A. and Mayo, G. D. An experiment in basic airborne electronics training time upon knowledge of radar maintenance. Technical Bulletin STB 67-12. U. S. Naval Personnel Research Activity, San Diego, California, 1966.

Lord, F. The measurement of growth. *Educational and Psychological Measurement*, 1956, 16, 421-437.

Manning, W. H. and DuBois, P. H. Correlational methods in research on human learning. *Perceptual and Motor Skills*, 1962, 15, 287-321.

McLean, M. L. Characteristics of the learning curve as a function of initial performance. Unpublished master's thesis, Texas Christian University, 1959.

Reynolds, B., and Adams, J. A. Psychomotor performance as a function of initial level of ability. USAF Human Resources Research Center Research Bulletin No. 53-39, October, 1953.

Roff, M., Payne, R. B., and Moore, E. W. A statistical analysis of the parameters of motor learning. USAF School of Aviation Medicine, Project No. 21-0202-0001, Report No. 1, February, 1954, 1-22.

Ruch, F. L. The method of common points of mastery as a technique in human learning experimentation. *Psychological Review*, 1936, 43, 229-234.

Rulon, P. J. Problems of regression. *Harvard Educational Review*, 1941, 11, 213-223.

Schoenfeld, W. N. and Cumming, W. W. Some effects of alternation rate in a time-correlated reinforcement contingency. *Proceedings of the National Academy of Sciences*, 1957, 43, 349-354.

Simrall, Dorothy. Intelligence and the ability to learn. *Journal of Psychology*, 1947, 23, 27-43.

Sorenson, G. A. The use of teaching machines in developing an alternative to the concept of intelligence. *Educational and Psychological Measurement*, 1963, 23, 323-329.

Spearman, C. E. *The abilities of man: their nature and measurement*. London and New York: Macmillan, 1927.

Stake, R. E. Learning parameters, aptitudes, and achievements. *Psychometric Monographs*, 1961, No. 9.

Stake, R. E. Toward a technology for the evaluation of educational programs. In R. W. Tyler, R. M. Gagné and Michael Scriven, *Perspectives of Curriculum Evaluation*, AERA Monograph 1. Chicago: Rand McNally, 1967.

Thomson, G. H. A formula to correct for the effect of errors of measurement on the correlation of initial values with gains. *Journal of Experimental Psychology*, 1924, 7, 321-324.

Thorndike, E. L. (with Bregman, E. O., Tilton, J. W., and Woodyard, E.). *Adult learning.* New York: Macmillan, 1928.

Thorndike, R. L. Regression fallacies in the matched groups experiment. *Psychometrika,* 1942, 7, 85-102.

Thorndike, R. L. *Personnel selection; test and measurement techniques.* New York: Wiley, 1949.

Thurstone, L. L. *A factorial study of perception.* Chicago: University of Chicago Press, 1944.

Tucker, L. Determination of generalized learning curves by factor analysis. In "Factor analysis and related techniques in the study of learning," edited by P. H. DuBois, W. H. Manning, C. J. Spies. Technical Report No. 7, ONR Contract Nonr 816(02), August, 1959, 143-168.

Underwood, Benton J. *Experimental psychology, an introduction.* New York: Appleton-Century-Crofts, 1949.

Wallen, N. E. Development and application of tests of general mental ability. *Review of Educational Research,* 1962, 32, 15-24.

Wells, F. L. Practice and the work curve. *American Journal of Psychology,* 1913, 24, 35-51.

Wimms, J. H. The relative effects of fatigue and practice produced by different kinds of mental work. *British Journal of Psychology,* 1907, 2, 153-195.

Wissler, C. The correlation of mental and physical tests. *Psychological Review Monograph Supplement,* 1901, No. 16.

Woodrow, H. The relation between abilities and improvement with practice. *Journal of Educational Psychology,* 1938, 29, 215-230.

Woodrow, H. The ability to learn. *Psychological Review,* 1946, 53, 147-158.

INDEX

22-401

PRINTED IN U.S.A.